Vegetarianism, Theosophy & Occultism

By C. W. Leadbeater
Annie Besant

Copyright © 2021 Lamp of Trismegistus. All rights reserved. No part of this publication may be reproduced or transmitted in any form or by any means, electronic or mechanical, including photocopying, recording, or by any information storage and retrieval system, without permission in writing from Lamp of Trismegistus. Reviewers may quote brief passages.

ISBN: 978-1-63118-593-9

Esoteric Classics

Other Books in this Series and Related Titles

The Hymns of Hermes by G R S Mead (978-1-63118-405-5)

Clairvoyance and Psychic Abilities by A Besant &c (978-1-63118-403-1)

Gnosis of the Mind by G R S Mead (978-1-63118-408-6)

Freemasonry and the Egyptian Mysteries by C. W. Leadbeater (978-1-63118-456-7)

Dreams: What They Are and Caused by C W Leadbeater (978–1–63118–570–0)

An Outline of Theosophy by C W Leadbeater (978-1-63118-452-9)

Paracelsus, the Four Elements and Their Spirits by M P Hall (978-1-63118-400-0)

Essays on Ancient Magic by Helena P Blavatsky (978-1-63118-535-9)

Essays on the Esoteric Tradition of Karma by A Besant &c (978-1-63118-426-0)

The Use of Evil by Annie Besant (978-1-63118-532-8)

Occult Arts by William Q. Judge (978-1-63118-559-5)

The Alchemical Catechism of Paracelsus by Paracelsus (978-1-63118-513-7)

Alchemy in the Nineteenth Century by Helena P Blavatsky (978-1-63118-446-8)

Qabbalistic Teachings and the Tree of Life by M P Hall (978-1-63118-482-6)

The Historic, Mythic and Mystic Christ by Annie Besant (978–1–63118–533–5)

The Hidden Mysteries of Christianity by Annie Besant (978–1–63118–534–2)

The Brotherhood of Religions by Annie Besant (978–1–63118–563–2)

The Religion of Theosophy by Bhagwan Das (978–1–63118–565–6)

Arcane Formulas or Mental Alchemy by W W Atkinson (978-1-63118-459-8)

The Machinery of the Mind by Dion Fortune (978-1-63118-451-2)

The Leadbeater Reader: A Selection of Occult Essays (978-1-63118-483-3)

Audio versions are also available on Audible, Amazon and Apple

Other Books in this Series and Related Titles

Applied Theosophy by Henry S Olcott (978–1–63118–592–2)

Higher Consciousness by C W Leadbeater (978–1–63118–591–5)

Theories About Reincarnation and Spirits by H P Blavatsky (978–1–63118–590–8)

The Use and Power of Thought by C W Leadbeater (978–1–63118–589–2)

Commentary on the Pymander by G R S Mead (978–1–63118–588–5)

Hypnotism and Mesmerism by Annie Besant (978–1–63118–587–8)

Spirits of Various Kinds by Helena P Blavatsky (978–1–63118–586–1)

The Hidden Language of Symbolism by Annie Besant (978–1–63118–585–4)

Eastern Magic & Western Spiritualism by Henry S Olcott (978–1–63118–584–7)

Spiritual Progress and Practical Occultism by H P Blavatsky (978–1–63118–583–0)

Memory and Consciousness by Besant & Blavatsky (978–1–63118–582–3)

The Origin of Evil by Helena P Blavatsky (978–1–63118–581–6)

The Camp of Philosophy: Studies in Alchemy by Bloomfield (978–1–63118–580–9)

The Testaments of the Twelve Patriarchs (978–1–63118–579–3)

Occult or Exact Science? by Helena P Blavatsky (978–1–63118–578–6)

Occultism, Semi-Occultism & Pseudo Occultism by A Besant (978–1–63118–577–9)

The Fourth-Gospel and Synoptical Problem by G R S Mead (978–1–63118–576–2)

On the Bhagavad-Gita by T Subba Row &c (978–1–63118–575–5)

What Theosophy Does for Us by C W Leadbeater (978–1–63118–574–8)

Spiritual Life for Man by Annie Besant (978–1–63118–573–1)

The Mysteries by Annie Besant (978–1–63118–572–4)

Audio versions are also available on Audible, Amazon and Apple

Table of Contents

Introduction...7

Vegetarianism and Occultism
By C. W. Leadbeater...9

Vegetarianism in the Light of Theosophy
By Annie Besant...41

Empirical Vegetarianism
By W. Wybergh...61

INTRODUCTION

The word "esoteric" can be difficult to define. Esotericism in general can be seen less as a system of beliefs and more as a category, which encompasses numerous, different systems of beliefs. It's a bit of juxtaposition, since the word "esoteric" indicates something that few people know about, while the term itself broadly covers numerous philosophies, practices, areas of study and belief systems.

In a greater sense, Esotericism acts as a storehouse for secret knowledge, which is often considered ancient (by *tradition, if not by fact),* passed down from generation to generation, in private. At various times in history, simply possessing the knowledge of some of these subjects, was considered illegal and a jailable offence, if discovered. This usually included such general topics as Alchemy, Pharmacology, Qabalah, Hermeticism, Occultism, Ceremonial Magic, Astrology, Divination, Rosicrucianism and so on. Collectively, these areas of study were often referred to as the esoteric sciences.

Sometimes, the outer garment of a subject isn't esoteric, while what is hidden beneath it, is. As an example, Freemasonry isn't necessarily esoteric by nature *(at least not anymore),* but certain signs, passwords and handshakes given to the candidate during their initiation, are in fact, esoteric, in the sense that they are hidden from the general public.

Today, in the twenty-first century, such topics are readily available at bookstores across the country, and numerous mainsteam publishers offer beginners guides and coffee-table volumes on many of these subjects, intended for mass appeal. Books like *"The Secret"* have turned previously arcane topics into household knowledge. All that being the case, however, it isn't to say that there still aren't buried secrets to uncover, ancient wisdom being ignored and forgotten mysteries to be explored. In fact, it is often that we are only able to further our own studies by standing on the shoulders of these disappearing giants.

Lamp of Trismegistus is doing its part to help preserve humanity's esoteric history by making some of these classics available to those students who are seeking to unearth the knowledge of these ancient colossi.

So, be sure to check other titles from our *Esoteric Classics* series, as well as our *Occult Fiction*, *Theosophical Classics*, *Foundations of Freemasonry Series*, *Supernatural Fiction*, *Paranormal Research Series*, *Studies in Buddhism* and our *Christian Apocrypha Series*. You can also download the audio versions of most of these titles from Amazon, Apple or Audible, for learning on the go.

VEGETARIANISM AND OCCULTISM
by C.W. Leadbeater

In speaking of the relation between vegetarianism and occultism, it may be well for us to begin by defining our terms. We all know what is meant by vegetarianism; and although there are several varieties of it, it will not be necessary to discuss them. The vegetarian is one who abstains from eating flesh-food. There are some of them who admit such animal products as are obtained without destroying the life of the animal, as, for example, milk, butter and cheese. There are others who restrict themselves to certain varieties of the vegetable - to fruit and nuts, perhaps; there are others who prefer to take only such food as can be eaten uncooked; others will take no food which grows underground, such as potatoes, turnips, carrots, etc. We need not concern ourselves with these divisions, but simply define the vegetarian as one who abstains from any food which is obtained by the slaughter of animals - of course including birds and fish.

How shall we define occultism ? The word is derived from the Latin *occultus*, hidden; so that it is the study of the hidden laws of nature. Since all the great laws of nature are in fact working in the invisible world far more than in the visible, occultism involves the acceptance of a much wider view of nature than that which is ordinarily taken. The occultist, then, is a man who studies all the laws of nature that he can reach or of which he can hear, and as a result of his study he identifies himself with these laws and devotes his life to the service of evolution.

How does occultism regard vegetarianism ? It regards it very favourably, and that for many reasons. These reasons may be divided into two classes - those which are ordinary and physical, and those which are occult or hidden. There are many reasons in favour of vegetarianism which are down here on the physical plane and patent to the eyes of any one who will take the trouble to examine the subject; and these will operate with the occult student even more strongly than with the ordinary man. In addition to these and altogether beyond them, the occult student knows of other reasons which come from the study of those hidden laws which are as yet so little understood by the majority of mankind. We must therefore divide our consideration of these reasons into two parts, first taking the ordinary and physical.

Even these ordinary reasons may themselves be sub-divided into two classes - the first containing those which are physical and as it were selfish, and secondly those which may be described as the moral and unselfish considerations.

First, then, let us take the reasons in favour of vegetarianism which concern only the man himself, and are purely upon the physical plane. For the moment we will put aside the consideration of the effect upon others - which is so infinitely more important - and think only of the results for the man himself. It is necessary to do this, because one of the objections frequently brought against vegetarianism is that it is a beautiful theory, but one the working of which is impracticable, since it is supposed that a man cannot live without devouring dead flesh. That objection is irrational, and is founded upon ignorance or perversion of facts. I am myself an example of its falsity; for I have lived without the pollution of flesh food - without meat, fish or fowl - for the last thirty-eight years and I not only still survive, but have been during all that time in remarkably good health. Nor am I in any way peculiar in this, for I know some thousands of others who have done the same thing. I know some younger ones who have been so happy as to be unpolluted by the eating of flesh during the whole of their lives; and they are distinctly freer from disease than those who partake of such things. Assuredly there are many reasons in favour of vegetarianism from the purely selfish point of view; and I will put that first, because

I know that the selfish considerations will appeal most strongly to a majority of people, though I hope that in the case of those who are studying Theosophy we may assume that the moral considerations which I shall later adduce will sway them far more forcibly.

WE WANT THE BEST

I take it that in food, as well as in everything else, we all of us want the best that is within our means. We should like to bring our lives, and therefore our daily food as a not unimportant part of our lives, into harmony with our aspirations, into harmony with the highest that we know. We should be glad to take what is really best; and if we do not yet know enough to be able to appreciate what is best, then we should be glad to learn to do so. If we think of it, we shall see that this is the case along other lines, as, for example, in music, art or literature. We have been taught from childhood that if we want our musical taste developed along the best lines we must select only the best music, and if at first we do not fully appreciate or understand it, we must be willing patiently to wait and to listen, until at length something of its sweet beauty dawns upon our souls, and we come to comprehend that which at first awakened no response within our hearts. If we want to appreciate the best in art we must not fill our eyes with the sensational broadsheets of police news, or with the hideous abominations which are miscalled comic pictures; but we must steadily look and learn until the mystery of the work of Turner begins to unfold to our patient contemplation, or the grand breadth of Velasquez comes within our power to understand. So too in literature. It has been the sad experience of many that much of the best and the most beautiful is lost to those whose mental food consists exclusively of the sensational paper or the cheap novel, or of that frothy mass of waste material which is thrown up like scum upon the molten metal of life - novelettes, serials, and fragments of a type which neither teach the ignorant, nor strengthen the weak, nor develop the immature. If we wish to unfold the mind in our children we do not leave them to their own uncultivated taste in all these things, but we try to help them to train that taste, whether it be in art, in music or in literature.

Surely then we may seek to find the best in physical as well as in mental food, and surely we must find this not by mere blind instinct, but by learning to think and to reason out the matter from the higher point of view. There may be those in the world who have no desire for the best, who are willing to remain on the lower levels and consciously and intentionally to build into themselves that which is coarse and degrading; but surely there are many who wish to rise above this, who would gladly and eagerly take the best if they only knew what it was, or if their attention was directed to it. There are men and women who are morally of the highest class, who yet have been brought up to feed with the hyenas and the wolves of life, and have been taught that their necessary dietary was the corpse of a slaughtered animal. It needs but little thought to show us that this horror cannot be the highest and the purest, and that if we ever wish to raise ourselves in the scale of nature, if we ever wish that our bodies shall be pure and clean as the temples of the Master should be, we must abandon this loathsome custom, and take our place among the princely hosts who are striving for the evolution of mankind - striving for the highest and the purest in everything, for themselves as well as for their fellow-men. Let us see in detail why a vegetarian diet is emphatically the purest and the best.

1. MORE NUTRIMENT

First: Because vegetables contain more nutriment than an equal amount of dead flesh. This will sound a surprising and incredible statement to many people, because they have been brought up to believe that they cannot exist unless they defile themselves with flesh, and this delusion is so widely spread that it is difficult to awaken the average man from it. It must be clearly understood that this is not a question of habit, or of sentiment, or of prejudice; it is simply a question of plain fact, and as to the facts there is not and there never has been the slightest question. There are four elements necessary in food, all of them essential to the repair and the upbuilding of the body, (a) Proteids or nitrogenous foods; (b) carbohydrates; (c) hydro-carbons or fats; (d) salts. This is the classification usually accepted among physiologists, although some recent investigations are tending to modify it to a certain extent.

Now there is no question that all of these elements exist to a greater extent in vegetables than they do in dead flesh. For instance, milk, cream, cheese, nuts, peas and beans contain a large percentage of proteids or nitrogenous matter. Wheat, oats, rice and other grains, fruits and most of the vegetables (except perhaps peas, beans, and lentils) consist mainly of the carbohydrates - that is, of starches and sugars. The hydro-carbons, or fats, are found in nearly all the proteid foods, and can also be taken in the form of butter or of oils. The salts are found practically in all food to a greater or less extent. They are of the utmost importance in the maintenance of the body tissues, and what is called saline starvation is the cause of many diseases.

It is sometimes claimed that flesh-meat contains some of these things to a larger degree than vegetables, and some tables are drawn up in such a way as to suggest this; but once more, this is a question of facts, and must be faced from that point of view. The only sources of energy in dead flesh are the proteid matter contained therein, and the fat; and as the fat in it has certainly no more value than other fat, the only point to be considered is the proteids. Now. it must be remembered that proteids have only one origin; they are organized in plants and nowhere else. Nuts, peas, beans, and lentils are far richer than any kind of flesh in these elements, and they have this enormous advantage, that the proteids are pure, and therefore contain all the energy originally stored up in them during their organization. In the animal body these proteids, which the animal has absorbed from the vegetable kingdom during its life, are constantly passing down to disorganization, during which descent the energy originally stored in them is released. Consequently what has been used already by one animal cannot be utilised by another. The proteids are estimated in some of these tables by the amount of nitrogen contained therein, but in flesh- meat there are many products of tissue-change such as urea, uric acid, and creatine, all of which contain nitrogen and are therefore estimated as proteids, though they have no food value whatever.

Nor is this all the evil; for this tissue-change is necessarily accompanied by the formation of various poisons, which are always to be found in flesh of any kind; and in many cases the virulence of these poisons is very great. So you will observe that if you gain any nourishment from the eating of dead flesh, you obtain it because during its life the animal consumed vegetable matter. You get less of this nourishment than you ought to have, because the animal has already used up half of it, and you have along with it various undesirable substances, and even some active poisons, which are of course distinctly deleterious. I know that there are many doctors who will prescribe the loathsome flesh diet in, order to strengthen people, and that they will often meet with a certain amount of success; though even on this point they are by no means agreed, for Dr. Milner Fothergill writes: " All the bloodshed caused by the warlike disposition of Napoleon is as nothing compared to the loss of life among the myriads of persons who have sunk into their graves through a misplaced confidence in the supposed value of beef-tea." At any rate, the strengthening results can be obtained more easily from the vegetable kingdom when the science of diet is properly understood, and they can be obtained without the horrible pollution and without all the undesirable concomitants of the other system. Let me show you that I am not in all this making any unfounded assertions; let me quote to you the opinions of physicians, of men whose names are well-known in the medical world, so that you may see that I have abundant authority for all that I have said.

We find Sir Henry Thompson, F.K.C.S., saying: "It is a vulgar error to regard meat in any form as necessary to life. All that is necessary to the human body can be. supplied by the vegetable kingdom ... The vegetarian can extract from his food all the principles necessary for the growth and support of the body, as well as for the production of heat and force. It must be admitted as a fact beyond all question that some persons are stronger and more healthy who live on that food. I know how much of the prevailing meat diet is not merely a wasteful extravagance, but a source of serious evil to the consumer." There is a definite statement by a well-known medical man.

Then we may turn to the words of a Fellow of the Royal Society, Sir Benjamin Ward Richardson, M.D.; he says: " It must be honestly admitted that weight by weight, vegetable substance, when carefully selected, possesses the most striking advantages over animal food in nutritious value. I should like to see a vegetarian and fruit-living plan put into general use, and I believe it will be."

The well-known physician, Dr. William S. Playfair, C. B., has said quite clearly: "Animal diet is not essential to man"; and we find Dr.F.J.Sykes, B.Sc., the medical official for St. Pancras, writing: "Chemistry is not antagonistic to vegetarianism, any more than biology is. Flesh food is certainly not necessary to supply the nitrogenous products required for the repair of tissues; therefore a well-selected diet from the vegetable kingdom is perfectly right, from the chemical point of view, for the nutrition of men."

Dr. Francis Vacher, F.R.C.S., F.C.S., remarks: "I have no belief that a man is better physically or mentally for taking flesh-food."

Dr. Alexander Haig, F.E.C.P., the leading physician of one of the great London hospitals, has written : " That it is easily possible to sustain life on the products of the vegetable kingdom needs no demonstration for physiologists, even if the majority of the human race were not constantly engaged in demonstrating it; and my researches show, not only that it is possible, but that it is infinitely preferable in every way, and produces superior powers, both of mind and body."

Dr. M. F. Coomes, in *The American Practitioner and News* of July, 1902, concluded a scientific article as follows: "Let me state first that the flesh of warm blooded animals is not essential as a diet for the purpose of maintaining the human body in perfect health." He goes on to make some further remarks which we shall quote under our next head.

The Dean of the Faculty of Jefferson Medical College (of Philadelphia) said: "It is a well-known fact that cereals as articles of daily food hold a high place in the human economy; they contain constituents amply sufficient to sustain life in its highest form. If the value of cereal food products were better known it would be a good thing for the race. Nations live and thrive upon them alone, and it has been fully demonstrated that meat is not a necessity."

There you have a number of plain statements, and all of them are taken from the writings of well-known men who have made a considerable study of the chemistry of foods. It is impossible to deny that man can exist without this horrible flesh-diet, and furthermore that there is more nutriment in an equal amount of vegetable than of dead flesh. I could give you many other quotations, but those above mentioned are sufficient, and they are fair samples of the rest.

2. LESS DISEASE

Second: Because many serious diseases come from this loathsome habit of devouring dead bodies. Here again I could easily give you a long list of quotations, but as before I will be satisfied with a few. Dr. Josiah Oldfield, M.E.C.S., L.R.C.P., writes: "Flesh is an unnatural food, and therefore tends to create functional disturbances. As it is taken in modern civilisations, it is infected with such terrible diseases (readily communicable to man) as cancer, consumption, fever, intestinal worms, etc., to an enormous extent. There is little need to wonder that flesh-eating is one of the most serious causes of the diseases that carry off ninety-nine out of every hundred people that are born."

Sir Edward Saunders tells us : "Any attempt to teach mankind that beef and beer are not necessary for health and efficiency must be good, and must tend to thrift and happiness; and, as this goes on I believe we shall hear less of gout, Bright's disease, and trouble with the liver and the kidneys in the former, and less of brutality and wife-beating and murder in the latter. I believe that the tendency is towards vegetarian diet, that it will be recognised as fit and proper, and that the time is not far distant when the idea of animal food will be found revolting to civilized man."

Sir Robert Christison, M.D., asserts positively that "the flesh and secretions of animals affected with carbuncular diseases analogous to anthrax are so poisonous that those who eat the product of them are apt to suffer severely - the disease taking the form either of inflammation of the digestive canal, or of an eruption of one or more carbuncles."

Dr. A. Kingsford, of the University of Paris, says: "Animal meat may directly engender many painful and loathsome diseases. Scrofula itself, that fecund source of suffering and death, not improbably owes its origin to flesh-eating habits. It is a curious fact that the word scrofula is derived from *scrofa*, a sow. To say that one has scrofula is to say that he has swine's evil."

In his fifth report to the Privy Council in England we find Professor Gamgee stating that "one-fifth of the total amount of meat consumed is derived from animals killed in a state of malignant disease"; while Professor A. Winter Blyth, F.R.C.S., writes:

"Economically speaking, flesh food is not necessary - and meat seriously diseased may be so prepared as to look like fairly good meat. Many an animal with advanced diseases of the lung yet shows to the naked eye no appearance in the flesh which differs from the normal."

Dr M. P. Coornes, in the article above quoted, remarks : We have many substitutes for meat which are free from the deleterious effects of that food upon the animal economy - namely, in the production of rheumatism, gout and all other kindred diseases to say nothing of cerebral congestion, which frequently terminates in apoplexy and venal diseases of one kind and another, migraine and many other such forms of headache, resulting from the excessive use of meat and often produced when meat is not eaten to excess. Dr J. H. Kellogg remarks: "It is interesting to note that scientific men all over the world are awakening to the fact that the flesh of animals as food is not a pure nutriment, but is mixed with poisonous substances, excrementitious in character, which are the natural results of animal life. The vegetable stores up energy. It is from the vegetable world - the coal and the wood - that the energy is derived which runs our steam engine pulls our trains, drives our steamships and does the work of civilisation. It is from vegetable world that all animals, directly or indirectly, derive the energy which is manifested by animal life through muscular and mental work. The vegetable builds up; the animal tears down. The vegetable stores up energy; the animal expends energy. Various waste and poisonous products result from the manifestation of energy, whether by the locomotive or the animal. The working tissues of the animal are enabled to continue their activity only by the fact that they are continually washed clean by the blood, a never-ceasing stream flowing through and about them, carrying away the poisonous products resulting from their work as rapidly as they are formed. The venous blood owes its character to these poisons, which are removed by the kidneys, lungs, skin and bowels. The flesh of a dead animal contains a great quantity of these poisons, the elimination of which ceases at the instant of death, although their formation continues for some time after death. An eminent French surgeon recently remarked that 'beef-tea is a veritable solution of poisons'. Intelligent physicians everywhere are coming to recognise these facts, and to make a practical application of them."

Here again you see we have no lack of evidence; and many of the quotations with regard to the introduction of poisons into the system through flesh-food are not from the vegetarian doctors, but from those who still hold it right to eat sparingly of corpses, but yet have studied to some extent the science of the matter. It should be remembered that dead flesh can never be in a condition of perfect health, because decay commences at the moment when the creature is killed. All sorts of products are being formed in this process of retrograde change; all of these are useless, and many of them are positively dangerous and poisonous. In the ancient scriptures of the Hindus we find a very remarkable passage, which refers to the fact that even in India some of the lower castes at that early period commenced to feed on flesh. The statement made is that in ancient times only three diseases existed, one of which was old age; but that now, since people had commenced to eat flesh, seventy-eight new diseases had arisen. This shows us that the idea that disease might come from the devouring of corpses has been recognised for thousands of years.

3. MORE NATURAL TO MAN

Third: Because man is not naturally made to be carnivorous, and therefore this horrible food is not suited to him. Here again let me give you a few quotations to show you what authorities are ranged upon our side of this matter. Baron Cuvier himself writes: "The natural food of man, judging from his structure, consists of fruit, roots and vegetables"; and Professor Eay tells us: "Certainly man was never made to be a carnivorous animal." Sir Richard Owen, F. R. C. S., writes: "Anthropoids and all the quadrumana derive their alimentation from fruits, grains and other succulent vegetable substances, and the strict analogy which exists between the structures of these animals and that of man clearly demonstrates his frugivorous nature."

Another Fellow of the Royal Society, Professor William Lawrence, writes: "The teeth of man have not the slightest resemblance to those of carnivorous animals; and whether we consider the teeth, the jaws or the digestive organs, the human structure closely resembles that of the frugivorous animals."

Once more Dr. Spencer Thompson remarks: "No physiologist would dispute that man ought to live on vegetarian diet "; and Dr. Sylvester Graham writes: "Comparative anatomy proves that man is naturally a frugivorous animal, formed to subsist upon fruits, seeds, and farinaceous vegetables."

The desirability of the vegetarian diet will of course need no argument for anyone who believes in the inspiration of the scriptures, for it will be remembered that God, in speaking to Adam while in the Garden of Eden, said : " Behold, I have given you every herb bearing seed which is upon the face of all the earth, and every tree in the which is the fruit of a tree yielding seed; to you it shall be for meat." It was only after the fall of man, when death came into the world, that a more degraded idea of feeding came along with it;

and if now we hope to rise again to edenic conditions we must surely commence by abolishing unnecessary slaughter performed in order to supply us with horrible and degrading food.

4. GREATER STRENGTH

Fourth : Because men are stronger and better on a vegetarian diet. I know that people say: "You will be so weak if you do not eat dead flesh." As a matter of fact this is untrue. I do not know whether there may be any people who find themselves weaker on a diet of vegetables; but I do know this, that in many athletic contests recently the vegetarians have proved themselves the strongest and the most enduring - as for example in the recent cycling races in Germany, where all those who took high places in the race were vegetarian. There have been many such trials, and they show that, other things being equal, the man who takes pure food succeeds better. We have to face facts, and in this case the facts are all ranged on one side, as against foolish prejudices and loathsome lust on the other. The reason was plainly given by Dr. J. D. Craig, who writes :

"Vigour of body is often boasted by flesh-eaters, particularly if they live mostly in the open air; but there is this peculiarity about them, that they have not the endurance of vegetarians. The reason of this is that flesh meat is already on the downward path of retrograde change, and as a consequence its presence in the tissues is of short duration. The impetus given to it in the body of the animal from which it was taken is reinforced by another impulse in the second one, and for these reasons what energy it does contain is soon given out, and there are urgent demands for more to take its place. The flesh-eater, then, may do a large amount of work in a short time if well-fed. He soon gets hungry, however, and when so becomes weak. On the other hand, vegetable products are of slow digestion; they contain all of the original store of energy, and no poisons; their retrograde change is less rapid than meat, having just commenced, and therefore their force is released more slowly with less loss, and the person nourished by them can work for a long time without food if necessary, and without discomfort. The people in Europe who abstain from flesh are of the better and more intelligent class, and the subject of endurance has been approached and thoroughly investigated by them. In Germany and England a number of notable athletic contests that required endurance have been made between flesh-eaters and vegetarians, with the result that the vegetarian has invariably come off victorious."

We shall find, if we investigate, that this fact has been known for a long time, for even in ancient history we find traces of it. It will be recollected that of all the tribes of Greeks the strongest and the most enduring, by universal admission and reputation, were the Spartans; and the simplicity of their vegetable diet is a matter of common knowledge. Think too of the Greek athletes - those who prepared themselves with such care for participation in the Olympian and Isthmian games.

If you will read the classics you will find that these men, who in their own line surpassed all the rest of the world, lived upon figs, nuts, cheese and maize. Then there were the Roman gladiators - men on whose strength depended their life and fame; and yet we find that their diet consisted exclusively of barley- cakes and oil; they knew well that this was the more strengthening food.

All these examples show us that the common and persistent fallacy that one must eat flesh in order to be strong has no foundation in fact; indeed the exact contrary is true. Charles Darwin remarked in one of his letters: "The most extraordinary workers I ever saw, the labourers in the mines of Chili, live exclusively on vegetable food, including many seeds of leguminous plants." Of the same miners Sir Francis Head writes: " It is usual for the copper miners of Central Chili to carry loads of ore of two hundred pounds weight up eighty perpendicular yards twelve times a day; and their diet is entirely vegetarian - a breakfast of figs and small loaves of bread, a dinner of boiled beans, and a supper of roasted wheat."

Mr. F. T. Wood in his *Discoveries at Ephesus* writes: "The Turkish porters in Smyrna often carry from four hundred to six hundred pounds weight on their backs, and the captain one day pointed out to me one of his men who had carried an enormous bale of merchandise weighing eight hundred pounds up an incline into an upper warehouse; so that with this frugal diet their strength was unusually great."

Of these same Turks Sir William Fairbairn has said: "The Turk can live and fight where soldiers of any other nationality would starve. His simple habits, his abstinence from intoxicating liquors, and his normal vegetarian diet, enable him to suffer the greatest hardships and to exist on the scantiest and simplest of foods."

I myself can bear witness to the enormous strength displayed by the vegetarian Tamil coolies of the South of India, for I have frequently seen them carry loads which astonished me. I remember in one case standing upon the deck of a steamer, and watching one of these coolies take a huge case upon his back and walk slowly but steadily down a plank to the shore with it and deposit it in a shed. The captain standing by me remarked with surprise, " Why, it took four English labourers to get that case on board in the docks at London ! " I have also seen another of these coolies, after having had a grand piano put on his back, carry it unaided for a considerable distance; yet these men are entirely vegetarian, for they live chiefly upon rice and water, with perhaps occasionally a little tamarind for flavouring.

On the same subject Dr. Alexander Haig, whom we have already quoted, writes: "The effect of getting free from uric acid has been to make my bodily powers quite as great as they were fifteen years ago; I scarcely believe that even fifteen years ago I could have undertaken the exercise in which I now indulge with absolute impunity - with freedom from fatigue and distress at the time and from stiffness next day. Indeed I often say that it is impossible now to tire me, and relatively I believe this is true." This distinguished physician became a vegetarian because, from his study of the diseases caused by the presence of uric acid in the system, he discovered that flesh-eating was the chief source of this deadly poison. Another interesting point which he mentions is that his change of diet brought about in him a distinct change of disposition - that whereas before he found himself constantly nervous and irritable, he now became much steadier and calmer and less angry; he fully realises that this is due to the change in his food.

If we require any further evidence, we have it close to our hand in the animal kingdom. We shall observe that there the carnivora are not the strongest, but that all the work of the world is done by the herbivora - by horses, mules, oxen, elephants and camels. We do not find that men can utilise the lion or the tiger, or that the strength of these savage flesh-eaters is at all equal to that of those who assimilate directly from the vegetable kingdom.

5. LESS ANIMAL PASSION

Fifth: Because the eating of dead bodies leads to indulgence in drink, and increases animal passions in man. Mr. H. B. Fowler, who has studied and lectured on dipsomania for forty years, declares that the use of flesh foods, by the excitation that it exercises on the nervous system, prepares the way for habits of intemperance in everything; and the more flesh is consumed, the more serious is the danger of confirmed alcoholism. Many experienced physicians have made similar experiments and wisely act on them in their treatment of dipsomaniacs. The lower part of man's nature is undoubtedly intensified by the habit of feeding upon corpses. Even after eating a full meal of such horrible material a man still feels unsatisfied, for he is still conscious of a vague uncomfortable sense of want, and consequently he suffers greatly from nervous strain. This craving is the hunger of the bodily tissues, which cannot be renewed by the poor stuff offered to them as food. To satisfy this vague craving, or rather to appease these restless nerves so that it will no longer be felt, recourse is often had to stimulants. Sometimes alcoholic beverages are taken, sometimes an attempt is made to allay these feelings with black coffee, and at other times strong tobacco is used in the endeavour to soothe the irritated, exhausted nerves. Here we have the beginning of intemperance, for in the majority of cases intemperance began in the attempt to allay with alcoholic stimulants the vague uncomfortable sense of want which follows the eating of impoverished food - food that does not feed.

There is no doubt that drunkenness and all the poverty, wretchedness, disease and crime associated with it may frequently be traced to errors of feeding. We might follow out this line of thought indefinitely. We might speak of the irritability, occasionally culminating in insanity, which is now acknowledged by all authorities to be a frequent result of erroneous feeding. We might mention a hundred familiar symptoms of indigestion, and explain that indigestion is always the result of incorrect feeding. Surely, however, enough has been said to indicate the importance and far-reaching influence of a pure diet upon the welfare of the individual and of the race.

Mr. Bramwell Booth, the chief of the Salvation Army, has issued a pronunciamento upon this subject of vegetarianism, in which he speaks strongly and decidedly in its favour, giving a list of no less than nineteen good reasons why men should abstain from the eating of flesh.

He insists that a vegetarian diet is necessary to purity, to chastity, and to the perfect control of the appetites and passions which are so often the source of great temptation. He remarks that the growth of meat-eating among the people is one of the causes of the increase of drunkenness, and that it also favours indolence, sleepiness, want of energy, indigestion, constipation and other like miseries and degradations. He also states that eczema, piles, worms, dysentery and severe headaches are frequently brought on by flesh diet, and that he believes the great increase in consumption and cancer during the last hundred years to have been caused by the corresponding increase in the use of animal food.

6. ECONOMY

Sixth: Because the vegetable diet is in every way cheaper as well as better than flesh. In the encyclical just mentioned Mr. Booth gives as one of his reasons for advocating it, that "a vegetarian diet of wheat, oats, maize, and other grains, lentils, peas, beans, nuts, and similar food is more than ten times as economical as a flesh diet. Meat contains half its weight in water, which has to be paid for as though it were meat. A vegetable diet, even if we allow cheese, butter and milk, will cost only about a quarter as much as a mixed diet of flesh and vegetables. Tens of thousands of our poor people who have now the greatest difficulty to make ends meet after buying flesh-food, would by the substitution of fruit and vegetables and other economical foods, be able to get along in comfort."

There is also an economic side of this question which must not be ignored. Note how many more men could be supported by a certain number of acres of land which were devoted to the growing of wheat, than by the same amount of land which was laid out in pasture. Think, too, for how many more men healthy work upon the land would be found in the former case than in the latter; and I think you will begin to see that there is a great deal to be said from this point of view also.

THE SIN OF SLAUGHTER

Hitherto we have been speaking of what we have called the physical and selfish considerations which. should make a man give up the eating of this dead flesh, and turn him, even though only for his own sake, to the purer diet. Let us now think for a few moments of the moral and unselfish considerations connected with his duty towards others. The first of these - and this does seem to me a most terrible thing - is the awful sin of unnecessarily murdering these animals. Those who live in Chicago know well how this ghastly ceaseless slaughter goes on in their midst, how they feed the greater part of the world by wholesale butchery, and how the money made in this abominable business is stained with blood, every coin of it. I have shown clearly upon irreproachable testimony that all this is unnecessary; and if it is unnecessary it is a crime.

The destruction of life is always a crime. There may be certain cases in which it is the lesser of two evils; but here it is needless and without a shadow of justification, for it happens only because of the selfish unscrupulous greed of those who coin money out of the agonies of the animal kingdom in order to pander to the perverted tastes of those who are sufficiently depraved to desire such loathsome aliment. Remember it is not only those who do the obscene work, but those who by feeding on this dead flesh encourage them and make their crime remunerative, who are guilty before God of this awful thing. Every person who partakes of this unclean food has his share in the indescribable guilt and suffering by which it has been obtained. It is universally recognised in law that *qui facit per alium facit per se* - whatsoever a man does through another he does himself.

A man will often say: "But it would make no difference to all this horror if I alone ceased to eat meat." That is untrue and disingenuous. First, it *would* make a difference, for although you may consume only a pound or two each day, that would in time amount to the weight of an animal. Secondly, it is not a question of amount, but of complicity in a crime; and if you partake of the results of a crime, you are helping to make it remunerative, and so you share in the guilt. No honest man can fail to see that this is so. But when men's lower lusts are concerned they are usually dishonest in their view, and decline to face the plain facts. There surely can be no difference of opinion as to the proposition that all this horrible unnecessary slaughter is indeed a terrible crime.

Another point to be remembered is that there is dreadful cruelty connected with the transport of these miserable animals, both by land and sea, and there is often dreadful cruelty in the slaughtering itself. Those who seek to justify these loathsome crimes will tell you that an endeavour is made to murder the animals as rapidly and painlessly as possible; but you have only to read the reports to see that in many cases these intentions are not carried out, and appalling suffering ensues.

THE DEGRADATION OF THE SLAUGHTERMAN

Yet another point to be considered is the wickedness of causing degradation and sin in other men. If you yourselves had to use the knife or the pole-axe, and slaughter the animal before you could feed upon its flesh, you would realise the sickening nature of the task and would soon refuse to perform it. Would the delicate ladies who devour sanguinary beefsteaks like to see their sons working as slaughtermen ? If not, then they have no right to put this task upon some other woman's son. We have no right to impose upon a fellow-citizen work which we ourselves should decline to do. It may be said that we force no one to undertake this abominable means of livelihood; but that is a mere tergiversation, for in eating this horrible food we are making a demand that *some one* shall brutalise himself, that *some one* shall degrade himself below the level of humanity. You know that a class of men has been created by the demand for this food - a class of men which has an exceedingly bad reputation. Naturally those who are brutalised by such unclean work as this prove themselves brutal in other relations as well. They are savage in their disposition and bloodthirsty in their quarrels; and I have heard it stated that in many a murder case evidence has been found that the criminal employed the peculiar twist of the knife which is characteristic of the slaughterman. You must surely recognise that here is an unspeakably horrible work, and that if you take any part in this terrible business - even that of helping to support it - you are putting another man in the position of doing (not in the least for your need, but merely for the gratification of your lusts and passions) work that you would under no circumstances consent to do for yourself.

Then we should surely remember that we are all of us hoping for the time of universal peace and kindness - a golden age when war shall be no more, a time when man shall be so far removed from strife and anger that the whole conditions of the world will be different from those which now prevail. Do you not think that the animal kingdom also will have its share in that good time coming - that this horrible nightmare of wholesale slaughter will be removed from it ? The really civilised nations of the world know far better than this; it is only that we of the West are as yet a young race, and still have many of the crudities of youth; otherwise we could not bear these things amongst us even for a day. Beyond all question the future is with the vegetarian. It seems certain that in the future - and I hope it maybe in the near future - we shall be looking back upon this time with disgust and with horror. In spite of all its wonderful discoveries, in spite of its marvelous machinery, in spite of the enormous fortunes that have been made in it, I am certain that our descendants will look back upon this age as one of only partial civilisation, and in fact but little removed from savagery. One of the arguments by which they will prove this will assuredly be that we allowed among us this wholesale, unnecessary slaughter of innocent animals - that we actually battened on it and made money out of it, and that we even created a class of beings who did this dirty work for us, arid that we were not ashamed to profit by the result of their degradation.

All of these are considerations referring only to the physical plane. Now let me tell you something of the occult side of all this. Up to the present I have made to you many statements - strong and definite, I hope - but every one of them statements which you, can prove for yourself. You can read the testimony of well- known doctors and scientific men; you may test for yourselves the economic side of the question; you may go and see, if you will, how all these different types of men contrive to live so well upon vegetarian diet. All that I have said hitherto is thus within your reach. But now I am abandoning the field of ordinary physical reasoning, and taking you up to the level where you have, naturally, to take the word of those who have explored these higher realms. Let us then turn now to the hidden side of all this - the occult.

OCCULT REASONS

Under this heading also we shall have two sets of reasons - those which refer to ourselves and our own development, and those which refer to the great scheme of evolution and our duty towards it; so that once more we may classify them as selfish and unselfish, although at a much higher level than before. I have, I hope, clearly shown in the earlier part of this lecture that there is simply no room for discussion in regard to this question of vegetarianism; the whole of the evidence and of the considerations are entirely on one side, and there is absolutely nothing to be said in opposition to them. This is even more strikingly the case when we come to consider the occult part of our argument. There are some students hovering round the fringes of occultism who are not yet prepared to follow its dictates to the uttermost, and therefore do not accept its teaching when it interferes with their personal habits and desires. Some such have tried to maintain that the question of food can make little difference from the occult standpoint; but the unanimous verdict of all the great schools of occultism, both ancient and modern, has been definite on this point, and has asserted that for all true progress purity is necessary, even on the physical plane, and in matters of diet, as well as in far higher matters.

In many books and lectures I have already explained the existence of the different planes of nature and of the vast unseen world all about us; and I have also had occasion to refer often to the fact that man has within himself matter belonging to all these higher planes, so that he is furnished with a vehicle corresponding to each of them, through which he can receive impressions and by means of which he can act. Can these higher bodies of man be in any way affected by the food which enters into the physical body with which they are so closely connected ? Assuredly they can, and for this reason. The physical matter in man is in close touch with the astral and mental matter - so much so that each is to a great extent a counterpart of the other. There are many types and degrees of density among astral matter, for example, so that it is possible for one man to have an astral body built of coarse and gross particles, while another may have one which is much more delicate and refined. As the astral body is the vehicle of the emotions, passions and sensations, it follows that the man whose astral body is of the grosser type will be chiefly amenable to the grosser varieties of passion and emotion; whereas the man who has a finer astral body will find that its particles most readily vibrate in response to higher and more refined emotions and aspirations. The man therefore who builds gross and undesirable matter into his physical body is thereby drawing into his astral body matter of a coarse and unpleasant type as its counterpart.

We all know that on the physical plane the effect of over-indulgence in dead flesh is to produce a coarse gross appearance in the man. That does not mean that it is only the physical body which is in an unlovely condition; it means also that those parts of the man which are invisible to our ordinary sight, the astral and the mental bodies, are not in good condition either. Thus a man who is building himself a gross and impure physical body is building for himself at the same time coarse and unclean astral and mental bodies as well. That is visible at once to the eye of the developed clairvoyant. The man who learns to see these higher vehicles sees at once the effects on the higher bodies produced by impurity in the lower; he sees at once the difference between the man who feeds his physical vehicle with pure food and the man who puts into it this loathsome decaying flesh. Let us see how this difference will affect the man's evolution.

IMPURE VEHICLES

If is clear that a man's duty with regard to himself is to develop all his different vehicles as far as possible, in order to make them finished instruments for the use of the soul. There is a still higher stage in which that soul itself is being trained to be a fit instrument in the hands of the Deity, a perfect channel for the divine grace; but the first step towards this high aim is that the soul itself shall learn thoroughly to control the lower bodies, so that there shall be in them no thought or feeling except those which the soul allows. All these vehicles therefore should be in the highest possible condition of efficiency; all should be pure and clean and free from taint; and it is obvious that this can never be so long as the man absorbs into the physical encasement such undesirable constituents. Even the physical body and its sense perceptions can never be at their best unless the food is pure. Any one who adopts vegetarian diet will speedily begin to notice that his sense of taste or of smell is far keener than it was when he fed upon flesh, and that he is now able to discern a delicate difference of flavour in foods which before he had thought of as tasteless, such as rice and wheat.

The same thing is true to a still greater extent with regard to the higher bodies. Their senses cannot be clear if impure or coarse matter is drawn into them; anything of this nature clogs and dulls them, so that it becomes more difficult for the soul to use them. This is a fact which has always been recognised by the student of occultism; you will find that all those who in ancient days entered upon the Mysteries were men of the utmost purity, and of course invariably vegetarian. Carnivorous diet is fatal to anything like real development, and those who adopt it are throwing serious and unnecessary difficulties in their own way.

I am well aware that there are other and still higher considerations which are of greater weight than anything upon the physical plane, and that the purity of the heart and of the soul is more important to a man than that of the body. Yet there is surely no reason why we should not have both; indeed, the one suggests the other, and the higher should include the lower. There are quite enough difficulties in the way of self-control and self-development; it is surely worse than foolish to go out of our way to add another and a very considerable one to the list. Although it is true that a pure heart will do more for us than a pure body, yet the latter can certainly do a great deal; and we are none of us so far advanced along the road towards spirituality that we -can afford to neglect the great advantage that it gives us. Anything that makes our path harder than it need be is emphatically something to be avoided. In all cases this flesh- food undoubtedly makes the physical body a worse instrument, and puts difficulties in the way of the soul by intensifying all the undesirable elements and passions belonging to these lower planes.

Nor is this serious effect during physical life the only one of which we have to think. If, through introducing loathsome impurities into the physical body, the man builds himself a coarse and unclean astral body, we have to remember that it is in this degraded vehicle that he will have to spend the first part of his life after death. Because of the gross matter which he has built into it, all sorts of undesirable entities will be drawn into association with him and will make his vehicles their home, and find a ready response within him to their lower passions. It is not only that his animal passions are more easily stirred here on earth, but in addition to this he will suffer acutely from the working out of these desires after death. Here again, looked at even from the selfish point of view, we see that occult considerations confirm the straight-forward common-sense of the arguments on the physical plane. The higher sight, when brought to bear upon this problem, shows us still more vividly how undesirable is the devouring of flesh, since it intensifies within us that from which we most need to be free, and therefore, from the point of view of progress, that habit is a thing to be cast out at once and for ever.

MAN'S DUTY TOWARDS NATURE

Then there is the far more important unselfish side of the question - that of man's duty towards nature. Every religion has taught that man should put himself always on the side of the will of God in the world, on the side of good as against evil, of evolution as against retrogression. The man who ranges himself on the side of evolution realises the wickedness of destroying life; for he knows that, just as he is here in this physical body in order that he may learn the lessons of this plane, so is the animal occupying his body for the same reason, that through it he may gain experience at his lower stage. He knows that the life behind the animal is the Divine Life, that all life in the world is Divine; the animals therefore are truly our brothers, even though they may be younger brothers, and we can have no sort of right to take their lives for the gratification of our perverted tastes - no right to cause them untold agony and suffering merely to satisfy our degraded and detestable lusts.

We have brought things to such a pass with our miscalled "sport" and our wholesale slaughterings, that all wild creatures fly from the sight of us. Does that seem like the universal brotherhood of God's creatures ? Is that your idea of the golden age of world-wide kindliness that is to come - a condition when every living thing flees from the face of man because of his murderous instincts ? There is an influence flowing back upon us from all this - an effect which you can hardly realise unless you are able to see how it looks when regarded with the sight of the higher plane. Every one of these creatures which you so ruthlessly murder in this way has its own thoughts and feelings with regard to all this; it has horror, pain and indignation, and an intense but unexpressed feeling of the hideous injustice of it all. The whole atmosphere about us is full of it. Twice lately I have heard from psychic people that they felt the awful aura or surroundings of Chicago even many miles away from it. Mrs. Besant herself told me the same thing years ago in England - that long before she came in sight of Chicago she felt the horror of it and the deadly pall of depression descending upon her, and asked: " Where are we, and what is the reason that there should be this terrible feeling in the air ? " To sense the effect as clearly as this is beyond the reach of the person who is not developed ; but, though all the inhabitants may not be directly conscious of it and recognise it as Mrs. Besant did, they may be sure that they are suffering from it unconsciously, and that that terrible vibration of horror and fear and injustice is acting upon every one of .them, even though they do not know it.

GHASTLY UNSEEN RESULTS

The feelings of nervousness and profound depression which are so common there are largely due to that awful influence which spreads over the city like a plague-cloud. I do not know how many thousands of creatures are killed every day, but the number is very large. Remember that every one of these creatures is a definite entity - not a permanent, reincarnating individuality like yours or mine, but still an entity which has its life upon the astral plane, and persists there for a considerable time. Remember that every one of these remains to pour out his feeling of indignation and horror at all the injustice and torment which has been inflicted upon him. Realise for yourself the terrible atmosphere which exists about those slaughterhouses; remember that a clairvoyant can see the vast hosts of animal souls, that he knows how strong are their feelings of horror and resentment, and how these recoil at all points upon the human race. They react most of all upon those who are least able to resist them - upon the children, who are more delicate and sensitive than the hardened adult. That city is a terrible place in which to bring up children - a place where the whole atmosphere, both physical and psychic, is charged with fumes of blood and with all that that means.

I read an article only the other day in which it was explained that the nauseating stench which rises from those Chicago slaughterhouses, and settles like a fatal miasma over the city, is by no means the most deadly influence that comes up from that Christian hell for animals, though it is the breath of certain death to many a mother's darling. The slaughterhouses make not only a pest-hole for the bodies of children, but for their souls as well. Not only are the children employed in the most revolting and cruel work, but the whole trend of their thoughts is directed towards killing. Occasionally one is found too sensitive to endure the sights and sounds of that ceaseless awful battle between man's cruel lust and the inalienable right of every creature to its own life. I read how one boy, for whom a minister had secured a place in the slaughterhouse, returned home day after day pale and sick and unable to eat or sleep, and finally came to that minister of the gospel of the compassionate Christ and told him that he was willing to starve if necessary, but that he could not wade in blood another day. The horrors of the slaughter had so affected him that he could no longer sleep. Yet this is what many a boy is doing and seeing from day to day until he becomes hardened to the taking of life; and then some day, instead of cutting the throat of a lamb or a pig he kills a man, and straightway we turn our lust for slaughter upon him in turn, and think that we have done justice.

I read that a young woman who does much philanthropic work in the neighbourhood of these pest houses declares that what most impresses her about the children is that they seem to have no games except games of killing, that they have no conception of any relation to animals except the relation of the slaughterer to the victim. This is the education which so-called Christians are giving to the children of the slaughterhouse - a daily education in murder; and then they express surprise at the number and brutality of the murders in that district. Yet your Christian public goes on serenely saying its prayers and singing its psalms and listening to its sermons, as if no such outrages were being perpetrated against God's children in that sinkhole of pestilence and crime. Surely the habit of eating dead flesh has produced a moral apathy among us. Are you doing well, do you think, in rearing your future citizens among surroundings of such utter brutality as this ? Even on the physical plane this is a terribly serious matter, and from the occult point of view it is unfortunately far more serious still; for the occultist sees the psychic result of all this, sees how these forces are acting upon the people and how they intensify brutality and unscrupulousness. He sees what a centre of vice and of crime you have created, and how from it the infection is gradually spreading until it affects the whole country, and even the whole of what is called civilised humanity.

The world is being affected by it in many ways which most people do not in the least realise. There are constant feelings of causeless terror in the air. Many of your children are unnecessarily and inexplicably afraid; they feel terror of they know not what - terror of the dark, or when they are alone for a few moments. Strong forces are playing about us for which you cannot account, and you do not realise that this all comes from the fact that the whole atmosphere is charged with the hostility of these murdered creatures. The stages of evolution are closely interrelated, and you cannot do wholesale murder in this way upon your younger brothers without feeling the effect terribly among your own innocent children. Surely a better time shall come, when we shall be free from this horrible blot upon our civilisation, this awful reproach upon our compassion and our sympathy; and when that comes we shall find presently that there will be a vast improvement in these matters, and by degrees we shall all rise to a higher level and be freed from all these instinctive terrors and hatreds.

THE BETTER TIME TO COME

We might all be freed from it very soon if men and women would only think; for the average man is not after all a brute, but means to be kind if he only knew how. He does not think; he goes on from day to day, and does not realise that he is taking part all the time in an awful crime. But facts are facts, and there is no escape from them; every one who is partaking of this abomination is helping to make this appalling thing a possibility, and undoubtedly shares the responsibility for it. You know that this is so, and you can see what a terrible thing it is; but you will say: "What can we do to improve matters - we who are only tiny units in this mighty seething mass of humanity?" It is only by units rising above the rest and becoming more civilised that we shall finally arrive at a higher civilisation of the race as a whole. There is a Golden Age to come, not only for man but for the lower kingdoms, a time when humanity will realise its duty to its younger brothers - not to destroy them, but to help them and train them, so that we may receive from them, not terror and hatred but love and devotion and friendship and reasonable co- operation. A time will come when all the forces of Nature shall be intelligently working together towards the final end, not with constant suspicion and hostility, but with universal recognition of that Brotherhood which is ours because we are all children of the same Almighty Father.

Let us at least make the experiment; let us free ourselves from complicity in these awful crimes, let us set ourselves to try, each in our own small circle, to bring nearer that bright time of peace and love which is the dream and the earnest desire of every true-hearted and thinking man. At least we ought surely to be willing to do so small a thing as this to help the world onward towards that glorious future; we ought to make ourselves pure, our thoughts and our actions as well as our food, so that by example as well as by precept we may be doing all that in us lies to spread the gospel of love and of compassion, to put. an end to the reign of brutality and terror, and to bring nearer the dawn .of the great kingdom of righteousness and love when the will of our Father shall be done upon earth as it is in heaven.

VEGETARIANISM IN THE LIGHT OF THEOSOPHY
by Annie Besant

The title of the lecture that I am to deliver to you tonight shows you, I think, the limitations which I practically impose upon both the subjects mentioned in it, so defining the limits of what I have to say. I am to speak to you on "Vegetarianism in the Light of Theosophy". Now, it is certain that you may argue for the vegetarian theory and practice from very many points of view. You may take it from the standpoint of physical health; you may take it along the physiological and chemical lines; you might make a very strong argument in its favour from the connection between it and the use, or rather the disuse, of strong liquor, because the use of alcohol and the use of meat are very closely connected with each other, and are very apt to vary together in the same individual; or you might take it from other standpoints, familiar, probably, to many of you, in the arguments that you road in vegetarian journals and hear from vegetarian speakers. So again with Theosophy. If I were going to deal with it by itself, I should be giving an impression of its meaning and doctrines, tracing for you, perhaps, the course of its history, advancing arguments as to the reasonableness of its general teaching, as to the value of its philosophy to man. But I am going to take the two subjects in relation to each other, and that relation means that I am going to try to bring to some of you, who very likely are already vegetarians, arguments along a line of thought that may be less familiar to you than those with which vegetarianism is generally supported. And I am going also to try to show to those of you who are not vegetarians that, from the Theosophical standpoint, there are arguments to be adduced, other than those which deal with the nourishment of the body, with chemical or physiological questions, or even with its bearing on the drink traffic — a line of thought entirely different from these, and valuable perhaps especially because of its difference; just as you might bring up fresh reinforcements to an army that is already struggling against considerable odds.

The vegetarianism that I am going to argue about tonight is that which will be familiar to all of you as the abstinence from all those kinds of food which imply the slaying of the animal, or cruelty inflicted upon the animal. I am not going to take up any special line of argument, such as those which may divide one vegetarian party from the other. I am not going to argue about cereals, nor about fruits, nor about the variety of diets which form so much of the discussion at the present time. I am going to take the broad line of abstinence from all kinds of animal food, and I am going to try to show the reasons for such abstinence which may be drawn from the teachings of Theosophy, which may be endorsed by that view of the world and of men which is known under this name.

I ought to say before putting the argument that, while I believe the argument I put to be perfectly sound from the standpoint of Theosophy, I have no right to pledge the Theosophical Society as a whole to the acceptance of that argument, for, as many of you know, we do not require from persons who enter the Theosophical Society their acceptance of the doctrines which are known under the general name of Theosophy. We only ask them to accept the doctrine of universal brotherhood, and to search after truth in the cooperative spirit, as it were, rather than in the competitive. That is, we require from our members that they shall not attack aggressively the religions or other views of their neighbours, but that they shall show the same respect to others as they expect others will show to them in the expression of their opinions. With that one obligation we are content. We do not try to force Theosophical views on those who enter. Those of us who believe them to be true have faith in the force of truth itself, and therefore we leave our members perfectly free to accept or to reject them. That being so, you will understand that in speaking I am not committing the Society. The views that I speak are drawn from the Philosophy which may or may not he held by any individual member of our union.

Now, the first line of argument to which I am going to ask your attention regarding vegetarianism in the light of Theosophy, is this: Theosophy regards man as part of a great line of evolution; it regards man's place in the world as a link in a mighty chain, a chain which has its first link in manifestation in the divine life itself, which comes down, link after link, through great hierarchies or classes of evolving spiritual intelligences, which, coming downwards in this fashion from its divine origin through spiritual entities, then involves itself in the manifestation that we know as our own world; that this world, which is but the expression of the divine thought, is penetrated through and through with this divine life; that everything that we call law is the expression of this divine nature; that all study of manifestation of law is the study of this divine mind in nature; so that the world is to be looked on, not as essentially matter and force, as from the standpoint of materialistic science, but essentially as life and consciousness involving itself for purposes of manifestation in that which we recognise as matter and as force.

Then, starting with this idea and tracing what we may call this involution of life to its lowest point, we come to the mineral kingdom; from that to the life working upwards again, as it were, in an ascending cycle instead of a descending — matter becoming more and more ductile under the force of this now evolving life, becoming more and more plastic — until from the mineral is evolved the vegetable. Then, as, working in the vegetable kingdom, matter becomes yet more plastic and therefore better able to express the life and consciousness which are working within it, you come to the evolution of the animal kingdom, with its more highly differentiated energies, with its growing complexity of organisation, with its increased power for feeling pleasure and pain, and, above all, with the increase of individualisation, these creatures becoming more and more of the type of individuals, becoming more and more separated, as it were, in their consciousness, beginning to show the germs of higher consciousness; this primary life, that lives in all, being able to express itself more completely in this more highly organised nervous system, and being, as it were, trained in that by more responses to the contacts from the external universe. Then, still climbing upwards, it finds a far, far higher manifestation in the human form, and that human form is animated by the Soul and by the Spirit — the Soul which through the body manifests itself as mind, and the Spirit which by the evolution of the Soul gradually comes into manifestation in this external universe.

Thus man, by virtue of this Soul that becomes self-conscious, by virtue of this higher evolution — the highest which exists in material form in our world — is, as it were, the highest expression of this evolving life; he ought, therefore, also to be the most perfect expression of this continually growing manifestation of law. Because of the will which develops itself in man, which has the power of choice, which is able to say "I will", or "I will not", which separates itself from the lower forms of living creatures by this very power of self-conscious determination, which, just because it is near the expression of the divine, shows those marks of thought, of spontaneous action, which are characteristics of the supreme life evolving itself in matter — just because of all that, man has a double possibility, a greater responsibility, a higher or a more degraded destiny. He has this power of choice. That law which in lower forms of life is impressed on the form and which the form obeys, as it were, by way of compulsion; the law which in the mineral world leaves no choice to the mineral atoms; which, in the vegetable world again, is a compulsory law, developing it along certain definite lines, without, as far as we are able to judge, much power of resistance;

which in the animal speaks as instinct, which the animal obeys, and obeys continually; that law, as we follow the general order, when it comes to deal with man, finds a change.

Man is the disorderly element in nature; man it is who, although he has higher possibilities, sets up discord in this realm of law; man it is who, just by virtue of his developed will, has the power of setting himself against law and holding his own, as it were, for a while against it. In the long run the law will crush him. Always when he sets himself against it, the law justifies itself by the pain which it inflicts; he cannot really break it, but he can cause disorder, he can cause disharmony, he can, by this will of his, refuse to follow out the highest and the best, and deliberately choose the lower and the worse road. And just because of that power the power of choice — he has higher possibilities than lie before the mineral, the vegetable, or the animal world. For it is a higher type of harmony to put oneself consciously into union with the law than it is to be simply an apparatus moved by it without the volition that consciously chooses the higher; and therefore man is in this position: he may fall lower than the brute, but he can also rise infinitely higher. Therefore, the responsibility comes upon him to be the trainer of the lower nature, the educator of the lower nature, the gradual moulder, as it were, of the world into higher forms of being and nobler types of life. And man, wherever he goes, should be the friend of all, the helper of all, the lover of all, expressing his nature that is love in his daily life, and bringing to every lower creature not only the control that may be used to educate, but the love also that may be used to lift that lower creature in the scale of being.

Apply then that principle of man's place in the world, vicegerent in a very real sense, ruler and monarch of the world, but with the power of being either a bad monarch or a good, and responsible to the whole of the universe for the use that he makes of the power. Take then man in relation to the lower animals from this standpoint.

Clearly, if we are to look at him in this position, slaying them for his own gratification is at once placed out of court. He is not to go amongst the happy creatures of the woods, and bring there the misery of fear, of terror, of horror, by carrying destruction wherever he goes; he is not to arm himself with hook and with gun, and with other weapons which he is able to make, remember, only by virtue of the mind which is developed within him. Prostituting those higher powers of mind to make himself the more deadly enemy of the other sentient creatures that share the world with him, he uses the mind, that should be there to help and to train the lower, to carry fresh forms of misery and destructive energy in every direction. When you see a man go amongst the lower animals, they fly from his face, for experience has taught them what it means to meet a man. If he goes into some secluded part of the earth where human foot has rarely trodden, there he will find the animals fearless and friendly, and he can go about amongst crowds of them and they shrink not from his touch. Take the accounts you will read of travellers who have gone into some district where man has not hitherto penetrated, and you will read how he can walk among crowds of birds and other creatures as friend with friends. And it is only when he begins to take advantage of their confidence to strike them down, only then, by experience of what the presence of man means to them, do they learn the lesson of distrust, of fear, of flying from his presence. So that in every civilised country, wherever there is a man, in field or in wood, all living things fly at the sound of his footstep; and he is not the friend of every creature but the one who brings terror and alarm, and they fly from his presence.

And yet there have been some men from whom there has rayed out so strongly the spirit of love, that the living things of field and forest crowded around them wherever they went; men like St. Francis of Assisi, of whom it is told that, as he walked the woods, the birds would fly to him and perch on his body, so strongly did they feel the sense of love that was around him as a halo wherever he trod. So in India you will find man after man in whom this same spirit of love and compassion is seen, and in the woods and the jungle, on the mountain and in the desert, these two men may go wherever they will, and even the wild beasts will not touch them I could tell you stories of Yogis there, harmless in every act of thought and life, who will go through jungles where tigers are crouching, and the tiger will sometimes come and lie at their feet and lick their feet, harmless as a kitten might be, in face of the spirit of love. And thus it might he with all things that live: thus it would be, if we were friend instead of foe. And though, in truth, it would now take many a century to undo the evil of a bloodstained past, still the undoing is possible, the friendliness might be made, and each man, each woman, who in life is friendly to the lower creatures, is adding his quota to the love in the world, which ultimately will subdue all things to itself.

Pass from that duty of man as monarch of the world to the next point which in Theosophical teaching forbids the slaughter of living things. Some of you may know that part of our teaching is that the physical world is interpenetrated and surrounded by a subtler world of matter that we speak of as "astral"; that in that, subtle matter — which may be called ether if the name be more familiar to you — forces especially have their home; that in that world you have the reflection and the imaging of what occurs on the material plane; that thoughts also take image there, just as actions are there reflected, and this astral world lies between the material world and the world of thought. The thought-world, full of the thoughts of men, sends down these potent energies into the astral world; there they take image, which reacts upon the physical. It is this which is so often felt by the "sensitive". When he comes into a special hall, a house, a city, he is able to tell you, by a subtle feeling that he may be unable to explain, something of the general characteristics of the atmosphere of that house, or hall, or city — whether to him it is pure or foul; whether to him it is friendly or hostile; whether it exerts upon him a healthful or a hindering influence. One of the ways in which you may recognise the working of this astral world is by connecting it in your thought, as science is beginning to connect the ether, with all magnetic currents, and with all electric action. Take, for instance, the action that a speaker has upon a crowd. That is dependent upon the presence of this ethereal matter in which magnetic forces work, so that a sentence which is spoken charged with the magnetism of the speaker has a wholly different effect upon those on whose ears it falls than if they read the same sentence in cold blood, as it is called, in a newspaper or a book. Why ? Because the force of the speaker, taking form in this subtle matter which is the medium between him and the hearers, sets it throbbing to his vibrations; his magnetism charges it, throws it into waves, and these waves strike upon the similar matter in the bodies of the hearers, and the wave sweeps right across the hall, and this vibration of a single thought for the moment makes all who are there feel its power alike, though they may not do so afterwards. Over and over again, in talking to people — talking, I mean, from the platform — when the magnetic force is strong, you will carry away the people you are talking to, although they may not agree with the arguments you are putting to them, and you will see somebody clapping madly in his applause who you know is antagonistic to the thought that you are then expressing. Meet him on the following day, and you will find him very angry with himself because he let himself be carried away for the moment. What has done it ? It is this magnetic sympathy, this throwing of ether into waves, which strike on him as they strike on others, and both his body and brain respond to the vibrations, and so for a time he is mastered by this magnetic power of the speaker.

Now, taking that — which is only an illustration, to show you what I mean by this astral matter and the way in which it is thrown into vibration by magnetic currents — think of astral matter for a moment from the standpoint of Theosophy as interpenetrating and surrounding our world ; then carry your thoughts to a slaughter-house. Try to estimate, if you can, by imagination — if you have not been unfortunate enough to see it in reality — something of the passions and emotions which there are aroused, not for the moment in the man who is slaying — I will deal with him presently — but in the animals that are being slain! Notice the terror that strikes on them as they come within scent of the blood! See the misery, and the fright, and the horror with which they struggle to get away even from the turning down which they are being driven! Follow them, if you have the courage to do it, right into the slaughter-house, and see them as they are being slain, and then let your imagination go a step further, or, if you have the subtle power of sensing astral vibrations, look, and remember what you see: images of terror, of fear, of horror, as the life is suddenly wrenched out of the body, and the animal soul with its terror, with its horror, goes out into the astral world to remain there for a considerable period before it breaks up and perishes. And remember that wherever this slaughtering of animals goes on, you are there making a focus for all these passions of horror and of terror, and that those react on the material world, that those react on the minds of men, and that anyone who is sensitive, coming into the neighbourhood of such a place, sees and feels these terrible vibrations, suffer under them, and knows whence they are.

Now, suppose that you went to Chicago — I take that illustration because it is one where I myself particularly noticed this effect. Chicago, as you know, is pre-eminently a slaughtering city; it is the city where they have, I suppose, the most elaborate arrangements for the killing of animals which human ingenuity has yet devised, where it is done by machinery very largely, and where myriads upon myriads of creatures are slaughtered week by week. No one who is the least sensitive, far less anyone who by training has had some of these inner senses awakened, can pass not only into Chicago, but within miles of Chicago, without being conscious of a profound sense of depression that comes down upon him, a sense of shrinking, as it were, from pollution, a sense of horror which at first is not clearly recognised nor is its source at once seen. Now, here I am speaking only of what I know. And, as it happened, when I went to Chicago, I was reading, as I am in the habit of doing in the train, and I did not even know that I was coming within a considerable distance of the town — for the place is so enormous that it stretches much farther than a stranger would imagine, and it takes far longer to reach the centre than one has any notion of — and I was conscious suddenly, as I sat there in the train, of this sense of oppression that came upon me; I did not recognise it at first, ray thoughts were anywhere but in the city; but it made itself so strongly felt that I began to look and to try to sense what it was that was causing this result; and I found very soon what the reason of it was, and then I remembered that I was coming into the great slaughter-house of the United States. It was as though one came within a physical pall of blackness and of misery — this psychic or astral result being, as it were, the covering that overspread that mighty town. And I say to you that for those who know anything of the invisible world, this constant slaughtering of animals takes on a very serious aspect, apart from all other questions which may be brought to elucidate it; for this continual throwing down of these magnetic influences of fear, of horror, and of anger, and passion, and revenge, works on the people amongst whom they play, and tends to coarsen, tends to degrade, tends to pollute. It is not only the body that is soiled by the flesh of animals, it is the subtler forces of the man that also come within this area of pollution, and much, very much of the coarser side of city life, of the coarser side of the life of those who are concerned in the slaughtering, comes directly from this reflection from the astral world, and the whole of this terrible protest comes from the escaped lives of the slaughtered beasts.

I said that there was this, apart from the men who slaughter. But can we rightly leave them out of consideration when we are dealing with the question of flesh-eating? It is clear that neither you nor I can eat flesh unless we either slay it for ourselves or get somebody else to do it for us; therefore, we are directly responsible for any amount of deterioration in the moral character of the men on whom we throw this work of slaughtering because we are too delicate and refined to perform it for ourselves. Now take the case of the slaughterer. I suppose no one will contend that it is a form of business which he himself would very gladly take up, if he be either an educated or refined man or woman — for I do not know why women should be left out of this, as they figure largely amongst meat-eaters. I presume that very few men and very few women would be willing to go and catch hold either of sheep or of oxen and themselves slaughter the creatures in order that they may eat. They admit that it has on the person who does it a certain coarsening influence. So much is that recognised by law that, certainly in the United States — I don't know if the law is the same here — no butcher is permitted to sit on a jury in a murder trial; he is not permitted to take part in such a trial, simply because his continual contact with slaughter is held to somewhat blunt his susceptibilities in that connection, so that all through the States no man of the trade of a butcher is permitted to take part as juryman in a trial for murder. That law is not confined to the States, but, as I say, I do not know if it is the law in England. This is very clear and definite: that if you go to a city like Chicago, and if you take the class of slaughtermen there, you will find that the number of crimes of violence in that class is greater than among any other class of the community; that the use of the knife is far more common, and this has been observed — I am speaking now of facts that I gathered at Chicago — it has been observed that this use of the knife is marked by one peculiar feature, namely, that the blow struck in anger by these trained slaughtermen is almost invariably fatal, because instinctively they give it the peculiar twist of the hand to which they are continually habituated in their daily killing of the lower animals. Now that, in Chicago, is recognised as a fact, but it does not seem to imply in the minds of the people any moral responsibility for their share in the evolution of this very uncomfortable type of human being. And so with the whole question of slaughtering in this city and anywhere else.

Has it ever struck you as a rule in ethics that you have no right to put upon another human being for your own advantage a duty that you are not prepared to discharge yourself? It is all very well for some tine and delicate and refined lady to be proud of her delicacy and refinement, to shrink from any notion, say, of going to tea with a butcher, to certainly strongly object to the notion of his coming into her drawing- room, to shrink altogether from the idea of consorting with such persons — "So coarse, you know, and so unpleasant". Quite so, but why ? In order that she may eat meat, in order that she may gratify her appetite; and she puts on another the coarsening and the brutalising which she escapes from herself in her refinement, while she takes for the gratification of her own appetite the fruits of the brutalisation of her fellow men. Now, I venture to submit that if people want to eat meat, they should kill the animals for themselves, that they have no right to degrade other people by work of that sort. Nor should they say that if they did not do it the slaughter would still go on. That is no sort of way of evading a moral responsibility. Every person who eats meat takes a share in that degradation of his fellow men; on him and on her personally lies the share, and personally lies the responsibility. And if this world be a world of law, if it be true that law obtains not only in the physical, but also in the mental and the moral and the spiritual world ; then every person who has a share in the crime has a share also in the penalty that follows on the heels of the crime, and so in his own nature is brutalised by the brutality that he makes necessary by his share in the results that come therefrom.

There is another point for which people are responsible in addition to their responsibility to the slaughtering class. They are responsible for all the pain that grows out of meat-eating, and which is necessitated by the use of sentient animals as food; not only the horrors of the slaughterhouse, but also the preliminary horrors of the railway traffic, of the steamboat and ship traffic; all the starvation and the thirst, and the prolonged misery of fear which these unhappy creatures have to pass through for the gratification of the appetite of man. If you want to know something of it, go down and see the creatures brought off some of the ships, and you will see the fear, you will see the pain, which is marked on the faces of these our lower fellow-creatures. I say you have no right to inflict it, that you have no right to be party to it, that all that pain acts as a record against humanity and slackens and retards the whole of human growth; for you cannot separate yourself in that way from the world, you cannot isolate yourself and go on in evolution yourself while you are trampling others down. Those that you trample on retard your own progress. The misery that you cause is, as it were, mire that clings round your feet when you would ascend; for we have to rise together or to fall together, and all the misery we inflict on sentient beings slackens our human evolution, and makes the progress of humanity slower towards the ideal that it is seeking to realise.

Looking at the thing from this broad standpoint, we get away from all the smaller arguments on which discussion arises, away from all questions as to whether meat nourishes or not, whether it helps the human body or not; and we take our ground fundamentally on this solid position: that nothing that retards the growth and the progress of the world, nothing that adds to its suffering, nothing that increases its misery, nothing that prevents its evolution towards higher forms of life, can possibly be justified, even if it could be shown that the physical vigour of man's body were increased by passing along that road. So that we get a sound standpoint from which to argue. Then you may go on, if you will, to argue that as a matter of fact the physical vigour does not need these articles of food; but I would rather take my solid stand on a higher ground: that is, on the evolution of the higher nature everywhere, and the harmony which it is man's duty to increase, and finally to render perfect in the world.

You may notice on all these points I have been arguing outside, as it were, the individual meat-eater; I am not, therefore, urging abstinence for the sake of personal improvement, for the sake of personal development, for the sake of personal growth. I have been putting it on the higher basis of duty, of compassion, of altruism, on those essential qualities which mark the higher evolution of the world. But we have a right also to turn to the individual and see the bearing on himself, on his body, on his mind, on his spiritual growth, which this question of meat-eating or abstinence from meat may have. And it has a very real bearing. It is perfectly true, as regards the body, when you look upon it as an instrument of the mind, when you look on it as that which is to develop into an instrument of the Spirit; it is perfectly true that it is a matter of very great importance what particular kind of nourishment you contribute to the body that you have in charge. And here Theosophy comes in and says: This body that the Soul is inhabiting is an exceedingly fleeting thing; it is made up of minute particles, each one of which is a life, and these lives are continually changing, continually passing from one body to another, so that you get a great stream as it were of particles going from body to body and affecting, as they fall on them, all these bodies, affecting them either for good or for evil. Science, remember, is also coming to recognise that as truth. Science, studying disease, has found that disease is constantly propagated by these minute organisms that it speaks of as microbes; it has not yet recognised that the whole body is made of minute living creatures that come and go with every hour of our life, that build our body today, the body of someone else tomorrow, passing away and coming continually, a constant interchange going on between these bodies of men, women, animals, children, and so on.

Now suppose for a moment you look on the body from that standpoint, first, again, will come your responsibility to your fellows. These tiny lives that are building your body take on themselves the stamp that you put upon them while they are yours; you feed them and nourish them, and that affects their characteristics; you give to them either pure or foul food ; you either poison them or you render them healthy; and as you feed them they pass away from you, and carry from you to the bodies of others these characteristics that they have gained while living in your charge; so that what a man eats, what a man drinks, is not a matter for himself alone, hut for the whole community of which that man is part; and any man who in his eating or in his drinking is not careful to be pure, restrained and temperate, becomes a focus of physical evil in the place where he is, and tends to poison his brother men and to make their vitality less pure than it ought to be. Here both in flesh and in drink the great responsibility comes in. It is clear that the nature of the food very largely affects the physical organism, and gives, as it were, a physical apparatus for the throwing out of one quality or another. Now the qualities reside in the Soul, but they are manifested through the brain and the body; therefore, the materials of which the brain and the body are made up is a matter of very considerable importance, for just as the light that shines through a coloured window comes through it coloured and no longer white, so do the qualities of the Soul working through the brain and the body take up something of the qualities of brain and body, and manifest their condition by the characteristics of that brain and that body alike.

Now, suppose that you look for a moment at some of the lower animals in connection with their food; you find that according to their food, so are the characteristics that they show. Nay, if you even take a dog, you find that you can make that dog either gentle or fierce according to the nature of the food with which you supply him. Now, while it is perfectly true that the animal is much more under the control of the physical body than the man; while it is quite true that the animal is more plastic to these outer influences than the man with the stronger self-determining will; still it is also true that, inasmuch as the man has a body and can only work through that body in the material world, he makes his task either harder or easier as regards the qualities of the Soul, according to the nature of the physical apparatus which that Soul is forced to use in its manifestations in the outer world. And if in feeding the body he feeds these tiny lives, which make it up, with food which brings into action, with them, the passions of the lower animals and their lower nature; then, he is making a grosser and a more animal body, more apt to respond to animal impulses, and less apt to respond to the higher impulses of the mind. For when he uses in the building of his own body these tiny lives from the bodies of the lower animals, he is there giving to his Soul as an instrument a vehicle which vibrates most easily under animal impulses. Is it not hard enough to grow pure in thought? Is it not hard enough to control the passions of the body?

Is it not hard enough to be temperate in food, in drink, and in all the appetites that belong to the physical frame? Has not the Soul already a difficult task enough, that we should make its task harder by polluting the instrument through which it has to work, and by giving it material that will not answer to its subtler impulses, but that answers readily to all the lower passions of the animal nature to which the Soul is bound ? And then, when you remember that you pass it on, that as you eat meat, and so strengthen these animal and lower passions, you are printing on the molecules of your own body the power of thus responding, you ought surely to train and purify your body, and not continually help it, as it were, to remain so responsive to these vibrations belonging to the animal kingdom. And as you do so you send them abroad as your ambassadors to your follow men, making their task harder, as well as your own, by training these tiny lives for evil and not for good ; and so the task of every man who is struggling upwards is also rendered harder by this increase of the molecules that vibrate to the lower passions. And while that is true in the most terrible degree of the taking of alcohol — which acts as an active poison, going forth from every one who takes it — it is also true of this animalising of the human body, instead of the ensouling and spiritualising of it; we are keeping the plane of humanity lower by this constant degradation of the animal self.

When you come then to think of the evolution of the Soul in yourself, what is your object in life? Why are you here ? For what are you living ? There is only one thing which justifies the life of man, only one thing that answers to all that is noblest in him and gives him a sense of satisfaction and of duty done; and that is when he makes his life a constant offering for the helping of the world, and when every part of his life is so regulated that the world may be the better for his presence in it and not the worse. In Soul, in thought, in body, a man is responsible for the use he makes of his life. We cannot tear ourselves apart from our brothers; we ought not to wish to do it, even if we could, for this world is climbing upwards slowly towards a divine ideal, and every Soul that recognises the fact should lend its own hand to the raising of the world. You and I are either helping the world upward or pulling the world downward; with every day of our life we are either giving it a force for the upward climbing or we are clogs on that upward growth; and every true Soul desires to be a help and not a hindrance, to be a blessing and not a curse, to be amongst the raisers of the world and not amongst those who degrade it. Every true Soul wishes it, whether or not it is strong enough always to carry the wish into act. And shall we not at least put before us as ideal that sublime conception of helping, and blame ourselves whenever we fall below it. whether in the feeding of the body or in the training of the mind?

For it seems to me, looking at man in the light of Theosophy, that all that makes life well worth having is this co-operation with the divine life in nature, which is gradually moulding the world into a nobler image, and making it grow ever nearer and nearer to a perfect ideal. If we could make men and women see it, if only we could make them respond to the thought of such power on their own side, if only they would recognise this divine strength that is in them to help in the making of a world, to share in the evolution of a universe, if they could understand that this world in theirs, placed as it were in their hands and in their charge, that the growth of the world depends upon them, that the evolution of the world is laid upon them, that if they will not help, the divine life itself cannot find instruments whereby to work on this material plane — if they would realise that, then, with very many falls, their faces would be set upward; with very many mistakes and blunders and weaknesses, still they would be turned in the right direction, and they would be gazing at the ideal that they long to realise. And so in mind and in body, in their work in the inner world of force as in the outer world of action, the one ruling idea would be: Will this act and thought of mine make the world better or worse, will it raise it or lower it, will it help my fellow men or hinder them? Shall the power of the Soul be used to raise or to lower? If that thought were the central force of life, even though forgetting it or failing, the Soul would again take up the effort and refuse to yield because it had so often failed. If we could all do that and think that, and win others to do it too, then sorrow would pass away from earth, the cries and the anguish and the misery of sentient existence would lessen; then from man, become one with divine law, would love radiate through the world and bring it into nobler harmony. And each who turns his face in that direction, each who purifies his own thought, his own body, his own life, is a fellow-worker with the inner life of the world, and the development of his own Spirit shall come as guerdon for the work he does for the helping of the world.

EMPIRICAL VEGETARIANISM
by W. Wybergh

Among all the side-shows (to speak somewhat colloquially) of Theosophy, there is perhaps none which so soon and so directly impresses its importance upon the neophyte as the question of vegetarianism and total abstinence, and in some form or other it seems destined to dog his footsteps long after he has, in practice, decided for himself whether he will or will not give up his conventional diet. For, to a serious student, this bare, broad question, however he answers it, appears to be but the point of departure for a number of trains of thought which, if he follows them up, speedily lead him into the wilderness of the half-known and the totally unknown.

By way of a preface, I must ask pardon of my readers if there appears to be a good deal of the personal element in this article. I write in a spirit of enquiry, in the hope of provoking a reply from some more advanced student. In South Africa, whence I write, Theosophy is still in its infancy, there are no older students at hand to refer to, and I have consulted without success all the literature on the subject which I have been able to lay hands upon, including, I think, most of that which has been published by the Theosophical Publishing Society. My difficulties may perhaps be partly due to personal idiosyncrasies, but I think that they are at any rate partly inherent in the subject and therefore of interest to others. If I use my own experience as an illustration, it is partly because one is on safer ground in doing so, and partly in the hope that perhaps this little bit of practical and autobiographical psychology may be of some interest, or at any rate that it may arouse some sympathy for my benighted condition.

To begin with, I should say that I practise both vegetarianism and abstinence from alcohol, and have not the slightest desire to do otherwise, except occasionally, in order to save inconvenience to myself or to others. In this particular case it is not that the spirit is willing but the flesh weak, for both spirit and flesh are perfectly willing, so that I fear that it is the intellect that is weak, or at any rate is unable to be convinced; in short I am unable to justify the faith that is in me either to myself or to others.

The stock arguments in favour of the practice divide themselves naturally under two heads: on the one hand the appeal to our love of animals and the sacredness of life, in effect that eating flesh is forbidden because it involves killing, and killing is bad ; and on the other hand the statement that abstinence is necessary if we would "purify" our vehicles and make them into better channels for the life of higher planes to flow through.

Speaking broadly, the first set of arguments appear to me invalid, and the second set, while perfectly valid, and corroborated by my own practical experience as far as it goes, do not seem to me to have been worked out in detail, even in the published works of Mrs. Besant and Mr. Lead beater, in such a manner as to carry intellectual conviction by a real explanation of what "purification" means, and *how* it is that abstinence from meat, rather than, let us say, from bread, brings about such purification.

I am reduced, therefore, to the very lame statement that I am a vegetarian and total abstainer because it appears to suit me, and because certain people in whom I have confidence have told me that I ought to be; whereas I should like *to* feel, as the advocates of the practice are apparently happy enough to do, that it was in support of some grand principle, and that the ensuing purification of the vehicle could be explained to the scoffer as, for instance, one explains the removal of dirt by the chemical action of soap, and not merely by recourse to "experimentum in corpore vili".

I have said that the arguments resting on love for animals and respect for life appear on the whole invalid to me, and I will endeavour to explain how this is. I do not think I am open to the charge of callousness, in fact I believe myself to be a very humane man. At any rate I have an intense dislike of causing pain to man or beast, indeed the sight or knowledge of suffering in others causes me the most acute nervous distress; yet I cannot say that physical life appears to me a very important thing, or that the deprivation of it can be considered a calamity. After all: "He who regardeth this as a slayer, and he who thinketh he is slain, both of them are ignorant".

If there is one thing that I seem to myself to have learned from Theosophical teaching and study, it is that death is a matter of indifference, and no calamity. Theosophy, while removing, I hope for ever, the fear of death for myself, has also removed the idea of any peculiar sanctity attaching even to human life in general. Life, my own included, seems to me a thing to be weighed in the balance, *pari passu* with any other consideration, or thrown into the scales when necessary for the attainment of any other object.

I see no reason, for instance, to regret my advocacy of a war which cost thousands of lives (some given willingly, some most unwillingly), but which was necessary in order to attain to certain results which *seemed* to *me* — rightly or wrongly, more important than many lives. The correctness or otherwise of my judgment does not affect the argument, any more than does the correctness or otherwise of the judgment of those who think a flesh diet useful to the maintenance of their health.

Now if my attitude with regard to human life is, as I hope it is, a right and reasonable one, surely it is not unreasonable when applied to the life or the happiness and well-being of animals ? If it is sometimes right to cause loss of human life in war, then surely it cannot be always wrong to deprive animals of life. Their life is surely of far less value to themselves or to the group-soul to which they belong, and there are no sorrowing relatives to consider. Those persons who think that their own health and well-being is of more consequence to the whole world than the life of a pigeon are probably not very far wrong, and if, even though they be mistaken, they think that the death of a pigeon conduces to their own well-being, they are not, it seems to me, to be condemned for killing it. On the other hand, it follows that others who, like myself, think that they are better without pigeon-pie, would be wrong in killing, and vegetarianism thus becomes a matter of individual opinion, based upon no very clear premises.

Of course the real issue is frequently, and even usually, obscured by those who appeal to compassion by the drawing of harrowing and no doubt only too true pictures of the cruelties (utterly needless and inexcusable) which are practised in slaughter-houses and in the business of the supply and transport of animals. I fully share their indignation and disgust, but the argument is not affected thereby. Is it not possible, moreover, that our clairvoyant investigators may have wrongly ascribed the effects which they have observed on the astral plane to the actual taking of life, when they should really be ascribed to these horrible, but only incidental, cruelties?

Again, we are told that slaughter brutalises the slaughterer, and that we have no right to acquiesce in the performance by others of actions from which we should shrink ourselves. This is a double-edged and far- reaching argument, for it is surely begging the question to say that it is the trade which produces the brutal man, and not the brutal man who makes an otherwise harmless trade brutal.

Now, as to facts, my own small experience of butchers certainly corroborates Colonel Thornton's (see "*In Defence of the Sportsman*", *Theosophical Review* for January, 1905), namely, that in moral character they do not appear to differ much from other men. My much larger experience of sportsmen (not Miss Ward's kind) is that they are to be reckoned among the most humane of my acquaintance, and that, far from becoming brutalised, the more experienced the hunter becomes, the keener he is about true sport, the less he cares for the extent of his bag, and the more he loves and respects the animals he hunts. Lest I should be accused of being loath to relinquish my favourite pursuit, and thus of being biased, I may here say that though I have been, I am no longer, a sportsman, chiefly owing to lack of time, and to other more absorbing interests, and partly owing to the same reasons which make me a vegetarian. As for the other kind (Miss Ward's kind) — the man who hunts tame animals, and breeds pheasants for the fun of knocking them over by the hundred — I should not call him a sportsman, and his proceedings appear to me not so much cruel as inane.

To return to the butcher, however, let us grant for the sake of argument that for *us* slaughter would be brutalising. I do not see that it can on that account be assumed to be wrong for the butcher, who may be, let us suppose, at a very much lower stage of evolution. It would no doubt be wrong to force a sensitive person into the trade, but surely the honest butcher, doing his duty according to his lights, is also treading the appointed path and merits neither our pity nor our condemnation. We accept from others many services which it is right for them to render and for us to accept, but which it would be wrong for us to undertake, because it is not our "job", and we have other more suitable work to do which cannot be done by others.

All that has been said so far is on the assumption that death is an evil, though a comparatively small one, but I do not think we have any right to assume that it is an evil at all. Evolution proceeds by the building up and dissolution of successive forms, but who shall say that the building up is necessary and "good", and the dissolution wanton and "evil" ? Both seem to be necessary and complementary to one another. It is said, however, that we have no right to take upon ourselves the responsibility of deciding when the form is ripe for dissolution. This, however, involves the assumption that we are the makers instead of the agents of destiny. The world is the field for countless interwoven yet independent evolutions. Each pursues its own course and incidentally becomes the instrument by which the evolution of others is carried on. It must be granted, of course, that the higher the organism involved the greater is the responsibility attached to action, and apparently it is on this principle that we are expected to shrink from killing the ox, while cheerfully slaughtering the grain and the fruit; yet there cannot, it seems to me, be much validity in an argument based upon the avoidance of responsibility. Let us meanwhile remember that inaction and indecision are just as binding as action and decision, and that: "Inaction based on selfish fear can bear but evil fruit". If it is too great a responsibility to kill, not only a man, but even a pigeon, how is it that we dare assume the responsibility of parentage ?

If, however, we confine ourselves to the less complicated questions of animal life, it still is not apparent to me that in this respect there is any difference in responsibility between the man who breeds domestic animals without a view to the butcher, or "preserves" wild ones without a view to the gun, and the man who butchers the first for food or shoots the others for sport; both actions are equal in interference with the operation of natural laws. In the case of the sportsman the interference is at a minimum, for all wild animals die violent deaths, and the sportsman merely constitutes himself one of the natural agencies which are always at work.

But there are not wanting those who maintain both that the deprivation of life is in itself an evil act, and also that under no circumstances are we entitled to benefit directly or indirectly by the loss of others, to sacrifice the lower to the higher, or, as perhaps they would put it, to do evil that good may come. I have the greatest sympathy with this uncompromising attitude, though I am by no means prepared to grant the assumption involved. To me this attitude seems to be bound up with all the best and noblest aspirations of mankind. I do not blame those who keep this ideal before their eyes because they do not practise what they preach, for the simple fact is that it is impossible to live in the world as now constituted, and at the same time to carry out these beautiful and true ideas in practice.

I do not think that anyone will seriously maintain that it is possible to live in the world and to refuse to countenance under any circumstances the drawing of advantage from the killing or suffering or loss of man or beast. We are asked to consider our responsibility for the murder of pigs and the morals of the family butcher, but do we realise how far the ramifications of the principle "another's loss, our gain" extend ? For it is impossible to confine the matter to the question of killing or not killing, meat or bread ; the principle extends far more deeply and widely than that. It would be tedious to give instances, we can all supply them for ourselves.

Nevertheless, I admit that the altruistic principle is both beautiful and true, nay, I affirm that its realisation is the one thing worth living for. And yet the way to this realisation is not, it seems to me, by appeals to prejudice, labelling killing "bad", vegetarianism "good", sport "cruel", vivisection "diabolical", nor yet by arguments so mixed up with emotion and vivid imagery as to blind instead of illuminating, but rather by the resolute determination to see things as they are and make the best of them, to alleviate where we cannot cure, to comprehend rather than to condemn.

I have put forward my own feelings as a very small contribution to the psychology of the subject, believing them to be in some degree representative of the ordinary kind-hearted man, who earnestly wishes to be as considerate to his younger brothers as the circumstances permit, but does not think that the interests and convenience of the grown man *ought* to be unduly sacrificed to those of the child.

I believe that I can and do love animals and my fellow men, while I am perfectly ready to acquiesce in the pain or injury either of them or myself for good cause shown, ff death be an injury, then I am ready to sacrifice either my life or theirs, whichever seems required least in the scheme of things, trusting that if I do wrong I shall learn by my mistake.

The best guess that I can make at the rights and wrongs of the matter is that consistent altruism is not possible on the physical plane by its very nature, since in physical matters it is plain that the more one has, the less there is for others, and the logical consequence would often be self-starvation. It is therefore vain and futile to aim at pure altruism here. We have to follow our own *dharma*, however beautiful and attractive the *dharma* of another, far beyond us, may appear, and part of the *dharma* of the physical plane is the preservation of the body, even at the cost of others.

In matters of desire and intellect, altruism is more and more possible and therefore worth aiming at, but it seems that it cannot be logically and completely practised until we have passed beyond the boundaries of selfhood. Meanwhile we have to turn the wheel of Life-Death, creating, preserving, and destroying, for God fulfils Himself in many ways. We are tied to the world-order, and it appears to me a true world-order, not a weltering chaos of selfishness and cruelty, even though it does involve the taking of life and of other things, and even though, by virtue of That within us, we may feel and often do feel with St. Paul that "to depart and be with Christ is far better". That time is not yet come for us, though even here and now, if we lift our eyes from the details which appear so sordid and selfish, viewed by themselves, we may vaguely sense the One.

It seems to me reasonable and natural, and therefore an aspect of the Divine, that we men must, when called upon, whether we like it or not, sacrifice our life and our all for country, principles, or in fact whatever in the great scheme transcends in importance our own individuality; it seems right that a general should sacrifice the lives of his men, sending, from his own position of perfect security, thousands to certain death, if thereby the lives of others, and among them his own more valuable life, may be preserved for his country's advantage. If they volunteer, it is well, but if they do not, he sends them just the same; in either case he loves and honours them, even as he slays them, for though they are humbler, less important, and therefore rightly sacrificed, yet are they not his brothers?

Even so is it right and just that the happiness, the welfare, even the lives of animals should be sacrificed to man. We are not called upon to attempt the impossible task of avoiding killing, but rather to love while we kill, accepting or requiring the sacrifice of physical life (if it be a sacrifice) and giving in return that assistance on a higher plane which we are able, and should be willing, to give.

A grateful country cannot reward on the physical plane the sacrifice of her sons, and we cannot repay the animals we kill, yet we can vicariously reward the whole animal kingdom and the group-souls functioning therein, by our love and gratitude for what they give us; we can ensure, by care and thoughtfulness, that no wanton pain or unnecessary sacrifice is imposed upon them; and, more important still, we can see to it that by our own single-minded devotion the sacrifice which we accept from those below us is accepted but for the purpose of making us in our turn better implements of the Divine Will.

The attempt which is constantly made by the (physical) altruists of the Theosophical Society to utilise as argument that which, as I have said, in its ultimate fullness seems to lie beyond the intellect altogether, must inevitably lead us into a maze of casuistry.

It will be said, however, I do not doubt, that my own arguments are just as casuistical as those to which they are opposed. At any rate I am deeply conscious of the possibility of some underlying fallacy — a consideration which ought also to afflict those who differ from me, even if it is at times forgotten. My arguments, nevertheless, represent "truth" to me for the present, until I find better ones.

And to those who may think me captious I will only say that it is not comfortable to feel that one differs not only from Mrs. Besant, Mr. Leadbeater, and other "seers", but also from the main body of Theosophists.

I cannot deduce vegetarianism as a rule of life from the principles here discussed, nor do the principles themselves, as I have endeavoured to show, appear to be beyond question. Nevertheless, from behind the mist of thought and argument I seem to obtain a glimpse of truth of which the intellectual aspect, filtered through my personality, appears as follows:

Standing with Arjuna on the field of Kurukshetra, the enquirer learns that killing is right and necessary; that death is no evil; that action binds not, but the desire for the fruit of action. He then who takes life or accepts any sacrifice from others must, if he would be blameless, do so not for his personal advantage as an object in itself, but in order that by the sacrifice he may become better fitted to do the work, great or small, which he has to do. And, again, the amount of the sacrifice that he may accept or require from others is measured by the extent to which he in his turn is ready to sacrifice himself. Here at any rate is no sense of separateness, which is Hate, but that emphasising of the "united Self" which we are told is Love.

Let us now turn to the other set of arguments, which, as I have said, appear to me valid, to be borne out by my own limited experience, but yet to be so obscure and incomplete as to justify the application of the epithet "empirical" to the practice of vegetarianism.

In the first place it may, I think, be assumed that the object aimed at, viz., the improvement of the vehicles of man, is a reasonable one. Of course for those who make of self-improvement an object in itself — whose only desire is to enjoy the advantages of a wider consciousness, and the extended powers that accompany it — the question is whether, and how far, the game is worth the candle.

No doubt in the earlier stages of human development evolution is helped forward by enlightened selfishness, when the choice, that is to say, is between enlightened and unenlightened selfishness only.

It is also true that among intellectual people there are many to whom superphysical consciousness seems a very desirable end in itself, who are prepared to go to far greater lengths than mere abstinence from flesh and alcohol in order to attain their object, and of such, I suppose, are the Brothers of the Shadow.

For my own part I confess that the possession of astral vision, for instance, as a personal acquisition, does not seem to differ intrinsically from the possession of very acute physical sight or hearing, or say the power of physical flight.

None of these powers have fallen to my lot, and though they are all no doubt very desirable and attractive, yet I feel that I can get along quite well without them, and there are other much more important things to think of. Even from the selfish point of view I don't see that one is likely to be the least happier for their attainment, but, as I have said, this is a matter of taste.

Far otherwise is it when that which is beyond words has once shown itself, for then the motive is neither to have nor to know, but to be; rather is there no motive in all, but a devouring, overmastering attraction, which no created thing can satisfy. There is then no question, no weighing of advantages or disadvantages, though there may be and is temporary negligence, temporary forgetfulness and temporary failure.

Such a man, seeking only to become a more perfect expression of the Divine Will, cannot but adopt vegetarianism or any other measure as his rule of life, if once he is convinced of its utility.

Yet the moving force that impels him, while quite different to the emotional or sentimental reasons which some would substitute for it, is also quite a different thing from the intellectual conviction which guides his efforts, and this "conviction" itself is for the ordinary man a very complex thing, made up of a number of elements which vary in proportion with different individuals.

Perhaps the three principal elements are personal experience, the *ipse dixit* of friends or recognised authorities, and logical scientific reasoning by which alleged facts are shown to be in harmony with general principles or with other facts already recognised as such. A fourth, less common, and for most people less trust worthy, is the inner super-rational conviction.

For many individuals the first and second, taken together, are sufficient; for all, the last is authoritative when fully felt; but for complete knowledge in the ordinary scientific sense — that is, knowledge which is not merely personal opinion — all the first three elements are essential.

The first is the cornerstone of science; the second, while it saves time, is also required to assure us that our ideas are objective as well as subjective; and the third is the keystone of the arch, without which our knowledge is merely a heterogeneous pile of provisional and isolated facts.

For my own part I fancy that my conviction of the value of vegetarianism *to me* depends a good deal on number one, a little on number two, a good deal more on number four, and scarcely at all on number three ; and in general it appears to me that while experience and authority on the subject abound, we have up to the present a most notable and lamentable deficiency of attempts to put in the keystone.

And yet it appears to me that it is only when thus coordinated that any fact or theory is fit to be published abroad outside the circle of students, or that it can bo deemed to have passed into the general heritage of mankind.

I think I have said enough to show that I do not minimise the value of the higher knowledge, but it is indubitable that that knowledge cannot be communicated to others, and that by substituting for it mere emotionalism the cause of vegetarianism actually loses ground and is on the way to degenerating into a mere fad.

It is of course more than likely that the actual method by which a so-called "impure" physical body prevents the manifestation through it of forces from higher planes is, and must for the present remain, entirely beyond our comprehension, and therefore that a completed "proof" of the value of vegetarianism is impossible.

In this case, however, I think we should be frankly told so, instead of being put off with the statement that these forces cannot act through "gross" aggregations of the matter of the various sub-planes, which is no explanation at all.

But short of that, there is much to be done in the way of describing in terms of atoms, motion, relative position, in short of mechanism, what are those physical conditions which as a matter of fact do hinder such manifestation.

Here again it adds nothing to our knowledge to be told that certain chemical compounds are " pure" when derived from wheat, and "impure" when derived from flesh, and it is evident that an adequate conception of the sense in which "pure" and "impure" are used is of the first importance.

If we bear in mind that we are dealing with the physical body only, the moral or religious meanings connoted by the word "purity" must be ruled out, and the word used in a physical sense. At once, however, we encounter a confusion of ideas in the descriptions usually given.

For instance, in "*Man and His Bodies*", page 18, Mrs. Besant speaks of a "pure and noble (physical) dwelling for the self", thus attributing to the physical body qualities which are emotional and intellectual, and which therefore, as it appears to me, can only be attributed to the astral and mental bodies; and throughout not only this manual but all the literature on the subject there appears to exist a similar looseness in the use of terms such as "impure","polluting", "refinement", "gross", "coarse", etc.

I am not now discussing the question as to whether, in addition to the physical action of "gross" food, there may or may not be some *direct* action between it and the astral body. It is hardly conceivable that the chemical combinations of the physical plane can directly affect astral matter; though, if it is true that all physical aggregates have their more or less permanent astral counterparts, such action might be imagined though hitherto not described.

In the strict physical sense, however, an "impurity" is merely an admixture of some ingredient other than the essential one, be it harmless or harmful for any particular purpose. Dirt, in fact, is matter in the wrong place, and to introduce an emotional element of disgust, etc., can only confuse the issue; for it would appear that there is nothing common or unclean, all matter as such being equally divine, "products of decomposition" being merely re-arrangements of physical atoms and molecules, and just as "clean" as anything else.

Admittedly some products of decomposition, called "carrion" as a term of opprobrium, are extremely unpleasant to the senses of most men, though I have seen Kaffirs and other fourth-race men eating it with every appearance of enjoyment and of advantage to their health. But surely it is part of the vegetarian argument that our senses are no sufficient guide to what is really good for our bodies, any more than our emotions are.

It must be, then, that flesh and alcohol introduce into the body matter which, though as "clean" as any other matter, is either harmful to the health or else (which is the crux of the matter) has some specific, but hitherto unspecified, physical quality, which, in some hitherto unexplained way, hinders the manifestation through the body of the life of the higher planes, and which is not possessed by matter of the same chemical composition derived from vegetables without the interposition of an animal's organism or manufacturer's still.

As to health, there is no doubt that opinions differ among medical men, in whose province alone the matter lies ; yet as a layman I must say that I have failed to notice that a moderate consumption of flesh or alcohol prejudices the health of the ordinary man or unfits him for his work. ,

In any case, if it is claimed to be a fact, the reasons for it have not, as far as I know, been worked out in such a way as to convince the general body of medical men that a real law of Nature has been discovered — such, for instance, as that explaining the action of oxygen on the blood through the lungs. The "fact" is therefore as yet only "theory", and the keystone is lacking.

But how, on broad lines, are the effects of flesh and alcohol on the physical body to be generalised as influencing the Higher Life ?

The answer, to be convincing, must be in terms of pure mechanism, dealing with physical differences in the arrangement or motions of physical atoms and molecules, classifying some such arrangements as useful, others as harmful.

It is just here that all explanation fails at present. If it is permissible to take the words "gross" and "coarse" in the purely physical sense, their use would represent about the only attempt hitherto made at such a classification. It would then appear that in flesh, the atoms or molecules of matter, whether in the solid, liquid, or gaseous state, are in a different physical state of aggregation from that in which the atoms or molecules of the same substances exist when they are derived from the vegetable kingdom, or that they induce such a different condition in the materials already composing the human body.

If this is so, the difference, being physical, would be capable of being detected in the laboratory, or at any rate of being explained to the intellect of the ordinary educated man. I am not aware that any such distinction has yet been recognised, or that, for instance, albumen derived from flesh can be distinguished from any other albumen, or even from that which has been recently produced by chemists from "inorganic" ingredients; and the same applies with still more force to the simpler chemical compounds, such as fats, sugars, acids, mineral salts, and water itself.

In short, it appears broadly as though hydrogen were always the same hydrogen, carbonic acid always the same carbonic acid, and so on, however they are generated, and whencesoever they are derived. Colour is given to this, the common idea, also by Mrs. Besant's well-known article on "Occult Chemistry", where, on the four higher physical sub-planes, the ultimate atoms are shown to combine in fixed numbers and definite arrangements to produce those simpler forms which, on the gaseous sub-plane, combine to form the various gases known to chemists.

The subject of "products of decomposition", regarded as a definitely harmful class of constituents of the body, has already been referred to, and it has been pointed out that decomposition is merely the name for a re-arrangement of atoms or molecules, generally in simpler forms, and often involving an addition of oxygen. But, if this is so, almost anything may be regarded as a "product of decomposition".

To take the particular case of alcohol, again eliminating all moral or religious questions, and confining ourselves to its physical constitution; alcohol is the name given to a whole class of chemical compounds of carbon, hydrogen, and oxygen; and ordinary, or ethyl, alcohol is a member of this class, intermediate in properties between methyl and butyl alcohol. Ethyl alcohol in practice is usually derived from the "decomposition" of sugar, which again is derived from starch. It represents, in fact, a stage in the oxidation of sugar, and a continuance of the process, with further oxidation, converts it into acid (vinegar for instance). Where then does the "impurity" lurk? It is presumably not in the original starch of sugar, nor in the oxygen; and if it were the *process* that is "impure", then vinegar might be expected to be still worse.

Again, although ethyl, or ordinary alcohol, is usually prepared in the manner just indicated, yet the alcohols generally can, in the laboratory, be prepared by quite other methods. Are they equally harmful when thus prepared?

If the word coarse, or gross, in its strictly physical sense, be a more correct way of characterising the peculiar objectionable quality, then we have to understand that the molecules, or the atoms composing the molecules, of alcohol are more closely or more loosely packed together than are those of sugar or vinegar, and that this does all the damage.

I have intentionally discussed the subject from the point of view of chemistry and physics, and not from that of physiology, because I have practically no knowledge of the latter science. It is possible that the latter aspect may be most important, but, at any rate, there must be a chemical and physical side as well, and what I chiefly aim at in any case is to get this matter of "gross", "coarse", "impure", etc., cleared up, because, after all, it is the kind of term almost exclusively used by those who have tried to give a scientific explanation of the effect of flesh and alcohol upon the Higher Life.

One solution of the difficulty as regards flesh has indeed suggested itself to me, only, however, to be abandoned. It occurred to me that the difference between, say, carbon derived from an animal and carbon from a vegetable might be due to differences in the state of development of the ultimate physical atoms of which the chemical element carbon is composed. That is to say, that in the case of vegetable carbon these atoms might have developed an extra set of spirillae as compared with those composing animal carbon.

On the other hand, as the animal kingdom is higher in the scale than the vegetable, the class of atoms composing animal bodies might be expected to be the more highly evolved of the two. As, however, again I see *this* argument opening up a vista of cannibalism, there seems to be something shaky about it too!

On the whole, I confess with sorrow that all the "explanations" hitherto given explain nothing to me, but rather obscure the subject with a mist of words; and again, ever lurking in the background of my mind, are the words of the Christ:

There is nothing from without a man that entering into him can defile him, but the things which come out of him, those are they that defile the man.

There is, however, one very important way in which it would appear that vegetarianism can affect the astral body or mental body directly, but, then, presumably the same effect might be produced in many cases, my own included, by a precisely opposite course. I refer to the disciplinary result of going without what one likes. This seems to be a real and easily understood advantage for all who aim at the Higher Life. In my case, however, even this satisfaction is denied me, for I detest, and always have detested, meat and alcohol, or rather, having always done so as a child and young man, I am now, after a short struggle with the acquired conventional habits of society, returning to my distaste for them with a constantly decreasing amount of effort, so that by this time it would be a real penance to eat a beefsteak or drink a glass of champagne.

This, however, is travelling beyond the physical plane altogether, and touching upon the great question of asceticism, which is much more far-reaching than mere vegetarianism, though little emphasis is laid upon it in the arguments of vegetarians.

Now, as regards experimental vegetarianism there is, of course, a very large body of testimony as to the advantages *believed* to have been derived from it. And in my own limited experience the practical effects of abstinence from flesh and alcohol seem to corroborate the teachings received. It is perfectly true that since, some few years ago, I began these practices, I have found my health improving, my brain growing clearer, my thoughts and passions more under control, my hold upon the things, good and bad, of this world somewhat looser and more independent. Occasional glimpses of what seem to be higher planes have also not been wanting — overtones, as it were, of the common things of this life, some beautiful beyond words, some painful and depressing.

This, however, is entirely vitiated as a criterion of the value of abstinence by the fact that at the same time as I adopted the latter as a rule of life I also began a very much stricter supervision over my thoughts, passions and physical activities than ever before, driven forward by the intellectual light that followed my first recognition of Theosophy in this life, and by the immense accentuation of the impulse toward the Higher Life which must follow upon an increased intellectual grasp of ways and means.

Now, whatever the influence of the body upon the mind may be, the influence of the mind upon the emotions and the physical body is quite undoubted. Accordingly I am quite unable to say how much, if any, of the result is due to vegetarianism, and how much to direct efforts upon higher planes. To obtain a test of any value, abstinence should be coupled with an absence of special effort towards the Higher Life, and the only place that occurs to me where these conditions are fulfilled is in our prisons ! At any rate it is clear that my private experience does not in itself warrant me in advocating vegetarianism as a principle.

As to the value of Authority in general, I have once or twice already been permitted by the kindness of the Editors to express my opinion in this REVIEW, so I will not go over the ground again. If my reason told me that vegetarianism was wrong, no authority would weigh against it. As it is, my reason merely says "not proven", and in such a case it appears a small thing to follow the directions of those who say they know; it can do no harm and may do good, and is not difficult anyhow.

I must, however, frankly confess that at bottom I am a vegetarian because I am made that way, and cannot do otherwise. I have a deep and entirely irrational conviction, binding for me, but worthless for anyone else, that abstinence *is* right, if one only knew why, and an equally irrational purpose to follow it whither it may lead.

www.ingramcontent.com/pod-product-compliance
Lightning Source LLC
LaVergne TN
LVHW041635070426
835507LV00008B/639